D0330895

A
season
with
mom

A season *with* mom

love, loss, and the
ultimate baseball adventure

Katie Russell
Newland

HARPER
HORIZON

A Season with Mom

Copyright © 2021 by Katie Russell Newland

All rights reserved. No portion of this book may be reproduced, stored in a retrieval system, or transmitted in any form or by any means—electronic, mechanical, photocopy, recording, scanning, or other—except for brief quotations in critical reviews or articles, without the prior written permission of the publisher.

Published by Harper Horizon, an imprint of HarperCollins Focus LLC.

Any internet addresses, phone numbers, or company or product information printed in this book are offered as a resource and are not intended in any way to be or to imply an endorsement by Harper Horizon, nor does Harper Horizon vouch for the existence, content, or services of these sites, phone numbers, companies, or products beyond the life of this book.

All photographs courtesy of the author and used with permission.

ISBN 978-0-7852-3889-8 (eBook)

ISBN 978-0-7852-3888-1 (HC)

Library of Congress Control Number: 2020942460

Printed in the United States of America

21 22 23 24 25   LSC   10 9 8 7 6 5 4 3 2 1

To those who love the game.
To those who have lost . . .
a parent.
their way.
hope.
To those on a healing journey looking to find . . .
themselves.
their purpose.
love.
To cancer survivors.
To dreamers.
To moms.
Especially the mom who loved me.
This book is for you.

Contents

Foreword by Peyton Manning   ix

Introduction   xiii

1   BEgin   1
2   BE Present   6
3   BE the Light   12
4   BElieve   17
5   BE Generous   23
6   BE Hopeful   31
7   BE Family   36
8   BElong   45
9   BE Understanding   51
10   BE Resilient   55
11   BE Communicative   61
12   BE Compassionate   67
13   BE Adventurous   75
14   BE Mindful   83
15   BE Ready   89
16   BE Happy   95
17   BEcome   103

18   BEhind the Scenes   110
19   BE Strong   117
20   BE Calm   125
21   BE Alert   131
22   BE Reflective   141
23   BE Grateful   147
24   BE Forgiving   153
25   BE Balanced   159
26   BE Still   167
27   BE Loyal   173
28   BE Open   181
29   BE in the Moment   187
30   BE   195

Epilogue: Extra Innings

   BE Patient   201
   BE Love   208
   BE Flexible   215

Acknowledgments   221
About the Author   227

Foreword

DEAR READER,

Congratulations on picking up this book of letters. Personally, I am a huge fan of letter writing. My mom always encouraged me and my brothers to send thank-you notes. Handwritten, of course!

Over the years, I've written countless letters. To children and adults facing illness, injury, or any personal hardship, I have shared words of encouragement and support. To former teammates and opponents, I have sent notes congratulating them on a great career. To those who lost a loved one, I have written to express my sympathy and let them know they are in my prayers.

And to family, friends, and fans, I have written to simply say, "Thank you."

Once I became a father, I began writing notes to my kids about the memories we were making—even before they were old enough to read them.

You might be wondering, *Why all of the letters?*

Let me tell you why.

Letters strengthen relationships. They are personal—often emotional—and can take the tone of congratulations, consolation, or gratitude. Unlike a quick text or email, handwritten letters take more time and effort. They leave a lasting impression on the recipient.

Letters have staying power. Think about a time you received a note from someone important in your life. If you're like me, you have a few of these stashed in the back of a drawer for safekeeping.

And one more thing I've learned about letters: the act of writing a letter can be as therapeutic for the writer as reading the letter is meaningful to the recipient. Whether we are on the giving or receiving end, letters can help all of us through the changing seasons of our lives.

In 2012, when I learned about my friend Katie's cancer diagnosis, I wrote her a letter. We have known each other from our earliest days and grew up as neighbors in New Orleans. I played many hours of football in the yard of her family's home on Seventh Street, with her brothers and mine. We went to high school together, where we both wore the white and kelly green of Isidore Newman School and proudly captained our respective athletic teams. On the same Michael Lupin Field where I played high school football, Katie earned MVP awards in soccer and softball.

Katie always had a fierce, competitive spirit, so I knew

cancer didn't stand a chance. I wasn't surprised one bit when I learned she beat the disease. Nor was I surprised that she came out of that fight with the determination to live out her dream to see every baseball stadium to honor her mom, who had passed from cancer several years earlier. When Katie sets out to do something, you can count on it.

And you can count on this book.

You likely opened these pages because you're a baseball fan or you were in search of the perfect gift for your mom. Good call, because this is a compelling story with America's pastime as the backdrop and an excellent gift.

You should know, though, you're going to get a lot more than that from *A Season with Mom*.

You're going to get a front-row seat to Katie's baseball stadium tour, as well as the intimate details of her cancer journey and a mother-daughter relationship. This insight will hit home for anyone who is a daughter, a son, a mother, or a father.

You're also going to get inspired. Maybe you've been putting your own dreams on hold. Maybe you're recovering from your own illness. Maybe you have lost someone you care about and are wondering how to stay connected.

After reading this book, you'll be eager to imagine your own amazing next season. What might it look like to follow through on your childhood dream? What could a note written today look like to your mom or dad, grandmother or grandfather, living or passed from this world? How good would it feel to send someone encouragement or let them know how grateful you really are?

A Season with Mom reignited a flame within me to never stop writing to people. I believe it will spark something inside you as well.

SINCERELY,
PEYTON

Introduction

I never really understood my mom. Her Cajun, New Orleanian mumble made it hard to understand her much of the time, yes, but that's not exactly what I mean. I never knew who my mom was. Her focus seemed to be on the people around her, preferring to listen rather than talk about herself. She would help a stranger before taking care of her own needs, and she chose to focus on the positive instead of "burdening" anyone with her reality. In constantly turning her attention to others, she somehow navigated through life without revealing much about herself. To me, or to the world.

At age sixty-nine, she died, leaving behind her six children: Hugh, Molly, Charlotte, Benjie, me, and Rachel. When she passed, so did my opportunity to truly understand her. I was thirty-two, and too busy rushing through my daily life and wrestling with the idea of losing my mom to pause and realize that the secret to understanding who *I* was could only be unlocked by knowing who *she* was.

Here's what I do know.

Her friends and, frankly, anyone who met her loved her. Anne Avegno Russell was magnetic and as competitive as they come—bridge, spades, Scrabble, croquet, Yahtzee. You name it; she played it. She kept a rotating stack of books by her bedside, and that provided all the evidence I needed at a young age to conclude she must be wicked smart. Although not professionally trained as a chef, she read cookbooks voraciously in our living room and channeled her creativity into one-of-a-kind dishes like "Sweetbreads Hugo" or "Crepes Mimi"—each named after a family member. Those dishes made their way into the mouths of endless patrons who frequented her small neighborhood restaurant with its evolving daily menu.

She spoke through food. When I had a tough day, she would say, "Want me to make your favorite pasta?" (For the record: fresh tomatoes and basil.) When Dad finally escaped New Orleans after Hurricane Katrina, one of the first things she said when she hugged him was, "Let's take you out for a steak dinner." Food was her love language.

Her other love language? Sports.

Mom could talk her way into a sports conversation with anyone, often surprising men. I would look up into the stands during my sporting events and find her in deep conversation, strategizing with my friends' dads. Soulful, intelligent, and intuitive, she connected with people instantly. But she remained largely out of reach for me. This was, in part, because I was the fifth of six kids and she worked full time as the owner of two restaurants. While she attended all of my sporting events, her schedule didn't allow her to be the "apple and a note in your lunch box" kind of mom or the person who sat next to me when I did my math flashcards at night.

But then there was baseball. I learned early on that if I wanted her attention, baseball was my ticket.

Lacking a local major league team in New Orleans, WGN, a Chicago-based television station, brought the Chicago Cubs into our Garden District home. And into Mom's heart, as well as mine. Baseball became the backdrop to my springs and summers. I loved opening the newspaper and reading the box scores in my mom's lap. I loved running into the house after school, dropping my book bag by the door, and racing to my mom's room. The game would already be on, and I would jump into her bed to catch up on the game's progress (and, more often than not, learn how badly the Cubs trailed). Most of all, I loved those quiet afternoons I spent with my mom—just the two of us—when nothing mattered but who stood at the plate.

Sometimes during the seventh-inning stretch or during Cubs off days, I sprinted to our yard and practiced throwing right below the room where Mom and I shared those lazy afternoons. I created a masking-tape box on the white brick wall for my strike zone, paced off a reasonable distance, and pretended to be on the mound at the Cubs' Wrigley Field. Most days, I'd find myself in the bottom of the ninth—guess I thought of myself as a relief pitcher and not a starter? Some days I threw for hours, and I'm surprised the noise didn't reverberate through Mom's room so loudly that she asked me to quit. I suppose she knew I had found my happy place. Baseball was our happy place.

We adored baseball. On the day we took a trip to Chicago to see our Cubs play, we even made a pact to visit all thirty major league ballparks. Alas, life had other plans for my mom, and we never lived out that dream.

Life had other plans for me too. I received my own cancer diagnosis three years after she died. Without her, I turned to baseball to get me through that trying time. Watching the Cubs play became my therapy, and two years after I completed my treatment, I knew exactly what I had to do.

⚾ ⚾ ⚾

Baseball has a way. You never know where it will take you. During the 2015 baseball season, the sport took me more than thirty thousand miles in search of my mom's legacy. On opening day, I set out to see all thirty Major League Baseball parks to fulfill my late mother's dream and to learn more about what the sport that bonded us for so long could teach me about her and our relationship.

Yes, this book is about baseball. But it's also a love story. It's a love story of a mother and daughter and our passion for the Chicago Cubs, the perennial underdog. It's a love story of the fans and the communities in which they reside. It's a love story of the pauses in life that give us an opportunity to self-reflect and to cultivate self-awareness—an opportunity to BE. And it's a love story of the unpredictable and complex world in which each of us lives. Ultimately, it's a reminder to you, the reader, that you don't have to love everything you go through, but you should know that everything you go through can bring you closer to your love. The strikeouts will always be there, but then so will the home runs. And even if the wait is 108 years (like it was for the Cubs to win the World Series), dreams really do come true.

WITH MOM AND DAD (1995)

BEgin

DEAR MOM,

It finally happened.

On what would have been your seventy-fourth birthday, I set out to accomplish what you dreamed of doing: visit every Major League Baseball park. Goose bumps blanketed my entire body, reminding me this moment meant more than any previous trip to the ballpark. Our long-awaited adventure had begun.

First up? Philadelphia, the city of our ancestors.

On the Phillies' opening day, the anticipation ran high for the players, for the fans, and, naturally, for me. I watched as a season ticket holder one row down meticulously opened his brand-new scorebook, eager to make his first pencil marks. Although he didn't say it, I knew what he was thinking: *Maybe this year we won't finish in last place. Maybe this year things will be different.* That's the beauty of a new baseball season. Each year, you have a chance to start over, to be better, to do something different.

Opening day in Philly marked my commitment to do something different for myself. After all, I had allowed baseball to pull this introverted, scared kid—the one who preferred to be at home watching a game over anything else—halfway across the United States. I'm sure you remember: you spent much of your life coaxing me to be adventurous. You drove me nuts urging me to go to the party where I would know no one; to go to camp like everybody else; to go to basketball tryouts, even though I would be the only girl there.

"Just go!" you'd say. "You never know—you might fall in love." That was the soundtrack of my life for thirty years . . . on repeat.

The thing about you, Mom, is that you loved jumping into things. You had six kids. You opened a restaurant with no training at the age of forty-two. Given only a few months to live, you flew to China. And how can we forget fantasy football? "Sure, I'll play," you told all of the men. And then you won the league. Without knowing how to turn on a computer.

You were spontaneous, a free spirit. I, on the other hand, have always been cautious and measured. While the unknown excited you, it frightened me. When I was the most anxious, you exuded confidence. Often, these differences between us left me feeling inadequate. But jumping into this adventure, I followed more than the baseball schedule to Philadelphia. I followed your lead.

As you've probably guessed, the journey began long before I packed my things, purchased my first "big-girl" camera, and set foot in Philadelphia. Do you remember our trip to Harry Caray's in Chicago? Do you remember where we sat? Harry's table. The table where the preeminent play-by-play Cubs announcer would sit when holding court in his namesake restaurant. At least that's what the hostess told us and, whether it was true or not, it worked. We all felt more special, practically skipping to our seats.

You let me pick one person to bring with me for my first visit to Chicago to see our beloved Cubs. Naturally, I picked my bestie since pre-K, Melissa, my only friend that shared our passion for the Cubbies. You also let me choose the restaurant. Potentially sitting in Harry's exact seat made even shy me sit up a little straighter and smile a bit wider. A definite buzz filled the air. It didn't take long to realize you were at your best, your personality shining like it often did when traveling. You wanted to do it all, try it all, be it all. Between nibbles of my burger, I watched those proverbial wheels turn in your head as you talked passionately about your love of baseball and your excitement for our first trip to Wrigley Field.

"Let's go see all the ballparks!" you shouted. Dad, who

didn't care much for baseball but came along because you told him to, displayed a similar enthusiasm (or at least pretended). Then came high fives all around and a shriek from you so loud it made the entire restaurant turn. I shrunk out of embarrassment, hoping my napkin would be large enough to disappear behind. I don't know any middle schooler who hasn't been embarrassed by her mom, and I was no exception. And this wasn't the first time. You embarrassed me a lot—sometimes I wondered if you enjoyed doing it.

After everyone in the restaurant quickly returned to their own conversations, I set aside my self-consciousness and considered what you had said. On the surface I thought, *Yesss!* On the inside, though, my stomach churned: *There's no way. It will cost too much. How do we even get to all of those games? There's no chance this is ever going to happen. This is another one of Mom's crazy dreams.*

It's a funny thing my anxiety and I like to do, preparing for disappointment and for things not to go exactly as I envision. I've mastered beating vulnerability to the punch. I've been doing it all my life. But at age thirty-eight, after watching you battle for your life and subsequently facing my own mortality, I decided to do something different.

When I made the decision to visit all thirty ballparks, I didn't incessantly worry about whether I could do them all or if I could afford it (that's what savings are for, right?)

or what people might think about me taking off on some big adventure by myself. Sure, I had a basic plan. Start on your birthday in Philadelphia, end in Chicago to watch our favorite team play, and complete the journey before October. That's it. Along the way, I may or may not have created a few spreadsheets. But the point is, I jumped right in, Mom. Like you always did. Like you always encouraged me to do. Off I went, doing exactly what you hoped we'd do together. I had no idea what it would become or where the journey would take me. For the first time since your death, I could hear your voice again: *"Just go, Katie. You might fall in love."*

Turns out you were right on this one.

Maybe you'd been right all along?

XO,

KATIE

BE Present

APRIL 12
OAKLAND ATHLETICS – OAKLAND COLISEUM

Dear Mom,

After Philadelphia, logistics led me to Oakland. I wanted to coordinate with my best friend and roommate from college, Michele, my biggest cheerleader, second only to you. She was the first to figuratively raise her hand and say, "I want to go to a game with you!" And since she lived in Northern California, it made perfect sense to meet up with her in Oakland.

The game that day extended into extra innings and managers faced even more decisions than usual, many of them based on timing. When to call the bullpen? When to send the runner? Of course, timing was critical to the players also. With each at bat, micromovements and milliseconds mattered for both hitter and pitcher. I had to step back and think about my own sense of timing that day too. What's worth taking time for? How does one choose to spend their time?

Michele and I crossed over the train tracks and San Leandro Street using a pedestrian footbridge entirely encased in a metal cage. Vendors sold bottled water from battered coolers with promises of cheaper prices than inside of the ballpark. The Oakland Coliseum stood as the last of the dual-purpose stadiums where the city's NFL team and MLB team shared the same field. This utilitarian design made walking up to a massive concrete stadium

a less-than-intimate entrance to the ballpark. Somehow, though, it didn't dull my excitement for what awaited beyond the industrial fencing.

An older gentleman at the gate told us we had narrowly missed out on the free giveaway. In the moment, it didn't seem like a big deal, until I noticed a group of twenty-year-olds in front of us walking into the stadium, admiring their new Oakland A's argyle socks and declaring in unison, "Sweet!" Their excitement sent me right back to school playground days when you realize your friends all have the cool new gadget and you somehow didn't get the memo. I, jokingly, blamed Michele for our untimely arrival.

Prior to the game, Michele took her time visiting with some employees outside of my hotel, who were painting the curb red—a shade not far removed from the one adorned by the Golden Gate Bridge on the other side of the bay. Her inexhaustible joie de vivre rivaled only yours, and, like you, she looooved to strike up conversations with anyone who crossed her path. Everyone within a one-yard radius has received a smile and a hello from her. Watching Michele over the years, always seizing the opportunity to connect and be present with people, made me think about you. I realized that being in Michele's company meant a part of you was with me; I smiled and shook my head slightly as I looked skyward at you.

Michele's eyes lit up and her pace increased as she

headed straight for the painters. She bent down to where they knelt and whispered something. The men smiled and then all three of them laughed. Before I could say, "Hey, we're going to be late for the game," the paint brush found its way to the palm of her hand. The sidewalk didn't stand a chance. The curb in front of the Oakland Airport Holiday Inn was about to become more colorful, compliments of Michele Bell. She couldn't pass up an opportunity to paint the town red, even if the delay cost us a pair of free knee-high socks with yellow-and-green diamonds. Timing really is everything, isn't it?

So, you might be wondering why I chose to go on this adventure in 2015, more than twenty-five years after inspiration struck that day at Harry Caray's.

As you may remember, in 2007, I moved to Austin to enroll in a PhD program at the University of Texas. I wanted to become smarter about how teachers are prepared. Over the next five years, the combination of my persistent perfectionism and a demanding program caused me to neglect virtually every aspect of my life that wasn't about successfully completing my degree.

Late-night fast-food runs were recurrent, missed weeks at the gym turned into months, and all-nighters became habitual. In 2012, nearing the end of my program and three years after your death, I was diagnosed with Hodgkin's lymphoma and melanoma. This reality forced me to hit the

Pause button on my graduate work and abruptly move to Houston for eight months of extensive chemotherapy and radiation treatment.

In 2013, when I had completed my treatment and returned to Austin and my "normal" life, I learned I had Lhermitte's sign: a rare side effect of radiation that impacts the spinal cord. Every time I walked or flexed my neck, an unpleasant electric-shock sensation radiated down my legs. I was thirty-six years old, thinking I had completed treatment and had my whole life ahead of me. But instead I became frustrated that I could barely walk much less exercise or join my friends for a spring afternoon at the lake. The worst part about it? I was alone in Austin and without you.

I channeled the push-through-anything attitude you displayed routinely as a restaurant owner and mother of six. Instead of wallowing in my unfortunate situation, I used it as an opportunity to get serious about finishing my degree. The sedentary lifestyle brought on by the Lhermitte's, and the large dose of steroids I was prescribed to minimize the side effects, kept me awake and at my computer for significant amounts of time. I liked to think of it as a little gift from the dissertation gods.

In December 2014, the Lhermitte's subsided, I received exciting news from my doctors that I was two years cancer free, and I defended my dissertation successfully, graduating with my PhD. All of these monumental events coinciding meant a transition loomed. Endings have a funny way of revealing new beginnings, and it felt like the perfect time to do some healing. While grateful to be alive, the emotional and physical roller coaster I'd been riding had taken its toll.

After missing out on an entire year of hanging out with friends, going to the movies, and eating out at restaurants, I wanted to live. I wanted to feel the sunlight on my face, to interact with strangers, to feel joy again. The pain of losing you right in the middle of my dissertation program left me with unresolved emotions. I needed to heal those wounds. I needed to make sense of my life and what had happened to me. It was time.

What better place for me to go than into the ballparks of the sport we have loved for most of our lives?

XO,
KATIE

3

BE the Light

APRIL 13

SAN FRANCISCO GIANTS – AT&T PARK

Hɪ Mᴏᴍ!

Michele joined me for another game. Lucky me! This time, we arrived early. We might have missed the argyle socks in Oakland, but we were *not* going to miss the World Series pennant giveaway and the opening-day celebration honoring the World Series Champion Giants. In fact, San Francisco won the trophy three times in the last five years. On the field before the game, a trifecta of Commissioner's Trophies shined bright in the afternoon light.

Opening day usually symbolizes a new start, a time-to-move-on mentality. But not that day. Opening day in 2015 gave the fans a chance to reflect on another successful San Francisco season. The Giants had clinched their most recent championship in Kansas City, and while the city had organized a parade for fans, this marked the first ballpark celebration since the Game Seven win in the fall. As you know, the Giants weren't my number one love, but they were Michele's. We both felt fortunate to be a part of the sold-out crowd.

During the pregame, the Giants' and visiting team's players and coaches lined up on the baselines, framing the three trophies and offering the crowd a powerful visual of teamwork. Even those uninterested in baseball know you can't win a World Series on your own. It takes a team. You can't have a pitcher without a catcher. Somebody has to wash all those uniforms! And it would be awfully hard to win a championship without the fans. This celebration

allowed the Giants organization an opportunity to thank the most ardent supporters.

Likewise, I knew I would need a great team if I intended to complete my thirty-ballpark tour. However, Mom, I didn't anticipate that your teammates would come out in full force when they heard about my journey. Your biggest fans wanted an opportunity to celebrate you and the championship life you led. Texts and emails poured in:

> Love following your travels in honor of my friend and your mother. She was special!
>
> ———————
>
> I *know* she is on each field with you that you visit, and because of *you*, we can all experience her again . . . thank you for that!

Shortly after my visit to the final ballpark, I reached out to a group of your life teammates, the McGehee School '59ers. Several of your former classmates (proud class of 1959) left New Orleans and moved permanently to Pass Christian. I planned a trip to see them, and Charlotte drove from Covington, Louisiana, to join me. Susan M., Bonnie, Bootie, Susan W., and Micey gathered on the back porch under the Mississippi moonlight, and I listened to your teammates tell tales of Anne.

Bonnie shared stories of your travels to China and London. "Everywhere we went, Anne *had* to read the local newspaper in addition to the *New York Times*." No one in the room seemed surprised. And we all laughed when Bonnie began describing your itty-bitty suitcase. "You could hardly call it a suitcase. It could easily have been mistaken for a toiletry bag!" It stood in stark contrast to Bonnie's self-proclaimed steamer trunk with which she traveled.

You preferred to travel light. Why let clothes bog you down when you've got things to do and people to meet? While you didn't realize you subscribed to a famous yogi's alleged philosophy—"Travel light, live light, spread the light, be the light"—that is exactly how you lived your life, Mom. You lit the flame within everyone who crossed your path.

Later in the evening, Susan W. looked me straight in the eye, shook her pointer finger, and proclaimed in her raspy twang, "You should know, there won't ever be anyone like Anne Russell. She was one of a kind."

Ain't that the truth?

You would have hated being the center of attention that night. I imagined you trying to change the subject from all the way up in heaven. I, on the other hand, cherished being surrounded by "Anne" stories. I learned a lot about you. One narrative, in particular, kept resurfacing.

"Anne was a really good listener. I could count on her to be there for me. Especially when life got hard."

So why didn't you let them return the favor when life got hard for you?

A private person, you didn't want to burden anyone. Once you learned your time on earth neared the end, you isolated yourself. You didn't allow your friends the opportunity to return the support you gave them. In the final game of your life, you pushed your team away. We granted your wish of having a Pass Christian beach service with only immediate family. But in so doing, your fans missed the chance to honor you.

Why?

My guess is that you didn't want people seeing you when you believed your light began to dim. I respect your decision. In fact, I'm the same way. As Dad says, "You don't get a pear from an apple tree." I did the same thing during my treatment—deliberately hiding from people until I knew I could win the match.

But what if you or I *had* let people in? What if we had allowed our darkness to be someone else's opportunity for light? What if we allowed people to support us when we were at our weakest and most vulnerable? Maybe that would have been the strong thing to do.

In the end, good teammates find a way. Yours embraced my ballpark adventure to honor you.

And even though you are gone, you should know that your light shines brighter than ever.

XO,
KATIE

4

BElieve

DEAR MOM,

I stepped into Dodger Stadium and into Major League Baseball's largest and third-oldest ballpark. A palm tree welcomed me with a wave as a slight wind blew through its fronds. I headed straight for the view at the Top of the Park, and Southern California didn't play coy. A 360-degree panorama revealed the San Gabriel Mountains, the tree-lined hills of Elysian Park, and downtown Los Angeles.

Some baseball analysts consider Dodger Stadium to be more favorable to pitchers than hitters. The high outfield walls, the depth of center field, and the California climate all conspire to keep balls in the park. Fans have watched an astonishing twelve no-hitters, while only two players have ever hit for the cycle there. This crossed my mind in the top of the second inning, as I witnessed a surprisingly conservative second bunt by the visiting team.

The bunt lost its allure in recent years. Baseball enthu-
siasts can thank sabermetrics, the empirical analysis of
baseball, for its decline. The bunt doesn't make sense sta-
tistically. But then again, you and I both know that baseball
is about more than numbers—even if many general managers these days seem to think otherwise.

Bunting is a small act of belief. It requires a player to
sacrifice an at-bat because he believes in his manager's

decision, not because he wants to bunt. Ask any kid who dreams of playing baseball. At no point in her dream does she think, *And I stepped up to the plate and bunted.* More likely than not, that kid is swinging for the fences.

Often, it's the little things in baseball, like a bunt, that make the difference in the outcome of a game. Ask legendary Yankees closer and Hall of Famer Mariano Rivera. The all-time leader in saves took the mound in the bottom of the ninth inning, up 2–1 during Game Seven of the 2001 World Series. With three outs, Rivera and the Yankees would win their fourth-straight title. Mark Grace (a favorite player of ours) led off with a single. The next batter squared around and bunted the ball right back to the pitcher. Rather than taking the easy out at first base, Rivera attempted to get the lead runner at second and overthrew the ball into center field. Rivera never recovered. Flustered, he gave up a double, hit a batter to load the bases, and served up a walk-off single. A wild celebration ensued as the Arizona Diamondbacks won their first-ever World Series title in only their fourth year of existence.

And it all started, in large part, because of a bunt.

Back in Dodger Stadium, I watched those players bunt and thought back to my decision to finally attempt our baseball dream and the small acts of belief it took to make our dream happen, Mom.

The weekend before the 2014 World Series started, I

chose to leave my computer and the final edits of my dissertation to travel from Austin to Houston and attend Oprah's
"The Life You Want" tour. Exhausted and overworked,
I knew some self-care would do me and my dissertation
good. Hugh joined me for a two-day event filled with inspi-
rational music, movement, and storytelling by some of the
greats (Deepak Chopra, Elizabeth Gilbert, and, of course,
Oprah).

All the way from my seat, I could feel Oprah's energy,
and it paled only in comparison to the crowd's collective
energy. When the sold-out Toyota Center audience began
to meditate, I felt the power in that stillness. The juxtaposi-
tion of the motivating cheers and the silence that followed
meant I could actually hear my thoughts: *What do you
want, Katie?*

I want to be healthy.
I want to find my person.
I want to inspire others.
I want to see my mom again and watch baseball with
      her.

I left Houston inspired and with a belief that, if I wanted
those things for my life, I had to ensure my choices aligned
with that vision.

I powered through the rest of my dissertation and

returned to MD Anderson Cancer Center for blood work and scans. By mid-December, I officially had the honor of being two years cancer free and Dr. Katie Russell!

Back in New Orleans for Christmas, I had a free afternoon while Dad worked and before Rachel's plane arrived. I walked to Canal Place—your favorite movie theater right in the heart of downtown New Orleans—to catch a matinee. This marked the first time I'd ever gone to the movies by myself. I had to believe that going alone didn't mean I lacked friends or social connectedness. It felt freeing as I took my seat among five others, in a virtually empty theater. My popcorn and I had plenty of space to sprawl out as we settled in to watch *Wild*—a movie I knew nothing about but one that friends had highly recommended.

I still had plenty of popcorn left when the big screen revealed a sign. It couldn't be coincidence that I chose a movie in which a daughter embarks on a journey to make sense of her life and her mother's death, right? By the time the credits rolled, I knew what I needed to do. Swap out the Pacific Crest Trail for thirty MLB ballparks, trade nature for some of the largest cities in North America, tweak another detail here or there, and *boom!* I had a plan for the next nine months.

I ordered a map of all the stadiums and stared at it for days, visualizing what a baseball tour might look like. I casually shared my idea with friends to gauge their reactions, but mentally, I'd already boarded the first flight—a small act of belief that no matter what people told me, I knew I could do it. While it seemed crazy at the time, I turned down the idea of applying for tenure-track assistant professor openings across the country—something I'd spent the last seven years working toward. I knew my savings would take a big hit and money would be tight, but if I wanted the life I'd outlined, I needed to take a risk. I would make our baseball dream a reality so we could watch baseball together again. I trusted my intuition.

During "The Life You Want" event, I met Oprah. I won't ever forget when she told the group not to see this as the day we took a picture with Oprah Winfrey but as the day we decided to start living the lives we wanted.

I listened. And I believed.

XO,
KATIE

5

BE Generous

APRIL 19

SEATTLE MARINERS – SAFECO FIELD

HOWDY MOM!

Ever since I decided to embark on this baseball journey, I couldn't wait to see a game with Rachel. The youngest in our family has a creative spirit and spunk suspiciously similar to yours. I knew that if she joined me for a game, her presence would make me feel like you scanned a ticket and joined us as well.

We hatched a plan to meet in San Francisco and ride the rails all the way up the Pacific coast to Seattle in time for us to see a Mariners game. You were a train enthusiast, with dreams to travel across Europe aboard the world's most luxurious train. You had so many dreams you didn't have a chance to fulfill. Rachel and I both felt that, in some small way, this would be fulfilling one of those dreams on your behalf. While the Coast Starlight was no Orient Express, it did help me understand why you romanticized trains. We felt close to the land and to the small towns that flew by outside the window, and we felt close to our fellow travelers.

The layout of our long-distance train encouraged interaction—two steps from our bunkroom to the bathroom, a forty-five-degree turn and five steps to the observation car. At mealtime, things got arduous: we had to walk *twenty* steps and go through *two* sets of sliding doors to reach the dining car. Some might consider traveling for twenty-four hours this way claustrophobic; we thought it was intimate.

No more than fifteen minutes after the train pulled away from Emeryville station, Rachel began introducing herself to our fellow passengers. Before you knew it, we gathered many of them around a small, oval table and began teaching them how to play Pass the Pigs.

"Games unite people," you taught us over the years, so it came as no surprise that it was the first thing Rachel and I did. Among the group: two retired flight attendants and their dog, Rocky; several European children on a family vacation; and a young Scandinavian couple eating their way across America, rating fast-food restaurants. (You would have loved the chart they created to score everything from service to freshness.)

We played games, laughed, drank mimosas, and swapped stories about where we had been in life and where we were headed. I imagined it was exactly the kind of experience that drew you to dream of train travel. People's life stories fascinated you and, even more, learning about which "chapter" they happened to be in. As Rachel and I stepped off the Coast Starlight in Seattle, our hearts sang from meeting such amazing people—and hearing such incredible life stories during our journey.

The next thing we knew, we stood outside Safeco Field, snapping photographs and giggling. Rachel laughed as I curled up, snake-style, inside of a giant baseball mitt, only realizing later that I was probably supposed to put my face through the hole. The oversized glove brought to mind a favorite quote, which I once read on Maya Angelou's Facebook page: "I've learned you shouldn't go through life with a catcher's mitt on both hands; you need to be able to throw something back." When I mentioned this to Rachel, together we remembered all of the ways you and Dad gave back to others.

You both chose caregiving professions. Dad practiced as an internist, and you taught history before becoming the chef I knew you as in my lifetime. You nourished the bodies and minds of everyone in your orbit. Your six children spent much of their lives surrounded by people some might refer to as strangers. But to you and Dad, these were merely people in need, and you were more than eager to give.

Remember the homeless man Dad invited to sleep in his eggnog-yellow Cadillac he kept parked outside of his

office? Rachel reminded me that, on several occasions, Dad asked her to take the man's clothes to the dry cleaner. (Meanwhile, I'm pretty sure our own clothes rarely made it to the dry cleaner.) At Thanksgiving meals, I looked around the table and saw, peppered among my siblings and relatives, faces I didn't recognize. Often, they were employees from your restaurant who didn't have anywhere to go for the holiday; in your world, neither food nor attention ran short for those who needed it.

And how could I forget Mardi Gras? Our proximity to the parade route meant our house had a revolving door on Fat Tuesday as you prepared enormous amounts of food for anyone who made their way into our dining room. On several occasions I found Dad outside helping a partygoer who had overindulged in more than the cotton candy sold on every street corner. One time, I discovered a man I'd never before seen lying on our couch, watching TV, eating some grillades and grits you prepared. After asking around, not a single person could identify him. Not a family member, a long-lost relative, a friend, or even a friend of a friend. Most would call him a stranger (and a rather presumptuous one at that!). When I asked you about the strange person in our living room, you assured me that he wasn't a stranger. In your eyes, no such person existed in this world.

Rachel and I have smiled often, retelling these stories, proud to call you our parents. The balance between helping people and taking care of yourself tipped way toward others. Whether I board a train with unknown passengers, walk past someone who seems to be struggling, or sit next to a stranger at a ballpark, I think about what you would do. You would want to know the person's story. You would want to speculate about why you had come into each other's lives. And, in many cases, you would want to know how you could help. When I decided to go on this adventure, I vowed to stop along the way and listen to people's stories. And if I was lucky enough to make it to all thirty ballparks, I would need to find a way to give back.

Rest assured, Mom, I kept my promise.

XO,
KATIE

6

BE Hopeful

APRIL 22

ARIZONA DIAMONDBACKS – CHASE FIELD

Hɪ Mᴏᴍ,

Growing up, I waited by the front door for Dad to come home at night. I'd sit with my back against the lower wooden half of the door, legs stretched out, my caramel-colored Wilson glove on my left hand, softball in my right. Every time I heard a noise, I popped up and peered over the wood and through the glass to see if it was him. Disappointed, I sat back down and continued throwing my ball into my glove, trying to work it in, the way Dad taught me.

I waited and hoped.

Eventually, I'd hear the car door shut, followed by a squeak of the iron gate. I'd yell, "Dad's home," yank at the brass knob, leave the door open behind me, and run out onto the porch. Before he ever stepped foot on the stairs, I looked down at him from the top. "Wanna play?"

"Hi, sugah—I'll throw a few with you."

I knew even then, and he confirmed later in life, that he'd barely had the energy to walk up the stairs. A long day at the office seeing patients, before heading to the hospital to make rounds, depleted him. By the time he came home, the last thing he wanted to do—after standing all day and listening to people's problems—was throw a softball.

But he always did.

We'd spread out on the porch, and as my arm strengthened over the years, I'd inch all the way back to the hanging swing. Sometimes when we threw, he caught with his bare hands. But on days he had more energy, he'd crouch in a catcher's stance with a mitt and shout, "Show me what you got!" I'd show off my windmill pitch. And he'd show off his flexibility and the durability of his suits, which he rarely seemed to take off.

After we played pitch and catch (as he referred to it), some nights he would reach into his coat pocket and toss me a pack of Raisinets. This last catch of the night meant one thing: on his way home from work, Dad had eaten dinner by himself at Casamento's, to have some alone time. I didn't have to ask what he ordered—spaghetti and daube and a half loaf of fried oysters with a pickle sliver.

⚾ ⚾ ⚾

By the end of the Diamondbacks game, thirteen hitters had crossed home plate. To put that in perspective, MLB teams averaged a tad over four runs per game that year. That's a lot of action at the plate, and it inspired my thinking about the importance of home, both in the game and in life.

Each at bat, players begin at home with the goal to get back there. In 1976, you brought me home shortly after my birth, and for the next fifteen years, we lived in our home located in the Garden District of New Orleans. Ever since we left, I've been trying to get back there, even if only in my mind.

I've often wondered what people think when they're on a tour of the historic district and they stand in front of our home. As a child, I watched them through the living room windows—the tour guides pointing and talking. Did they see it as more than a house? Did they see past the Corinthian columns and the century-old architecture and realize that the porch held stories of a family? Stories of a daughter and her dad playing pitch and catch?

At least one person saw it as something more. A local artist walking through the neighborhood.

One night, while scanning Instagram, a splash of New Orleans in the form of a painting caught my eye. I love art almost as much as baseball, so I searched for the artist's account. As I scrolled through his colorful and whimsical oil paintings, I noticed a photograph. A familiar house. The artist had snapped a picture of our home. I immediately commented on the post and inquired about whether he had painted it. "That's the house I grew up in," I told him. And he responded right away.

Nightfall in the Garden District now hangs in my home in Austin. He captured the front door I used to lean up against, he captured the shutters I played hide-and-seek behind, and he captured my favorite oak tree. With vibrant dusk colors, he captured the magic of our home. When I pass the painting on the way to the kitchen, my thoughts go to those nights on that porch playing catch with Dad, and I feel close to him. Something about playing catch with a round ball and a leather glove shortens the emotional distance between a father and his child—in the moment and, as it turns out, for many years to come.

Twenty-five years after porch nights with Dad and two months prior to my baseball odyssey, we received a call from a Charleston, South Carolina, hospital. Dad had suffered a massive heart attack while on vacation. Mom, your kids dropped everything and hopped in cars and on flights to be by his side. I'll spare you the traumatic details, but the doctor delivered a bleak prognosis. After surgery and many days in the ICU, the doctors decided to pull him off of the ventilator. The cardiologist on staff that day sat us down and made it clear that if they extubated him and he didn't start breathing on his own, they couldn't intubate him again.

As you know, Dad told us many years ago of his do-not-resuscitate wishes.

I waited by the ICU door, wondering if Dad would come home. Instead of my glove, I held my tear-soaked phone. I wore a week of no sleep and anxiety across my face. I wondered, *What would Dad do for his patients and their caregivers in this circumstance?*

He would ease their pain and give them hope. I decided to take a page out of Dad's playbook. I began to substitute my fear with hope. I realized that no matter what his lungs and heart decided to do, no matter what happened in that hospital room, Dad *would* go home. One way or another.

After what felt like hours, the doctor came into the waiting room, removed his mask, and delivered the news.

Dad would live to play another day of pitch and catch.

XO,

KATIE

7

BE Family

APRIL 25

TAMPA BAY RAYS – TROPICANA FIELD

Dear Mom,

I have a distinct memory of the time I crawled into my closet and shut the sliding door behind me so no one would hear me cry. It wasn't one of those teardrops-trickling-down-your-face cries; it was a loud, wailing, devastated kind of cry. The kind that leaves you with a stuffed-up nose and has you wondering two days later where you picked up a cold. My entire twelve-year-old world crumbled.

Ella Mae had left me.

I found myself thinking of Ella during my time in Tampa Bay. In this game, between the Toronto Blue Jays and the Rays, both American League teams naturally had designated hitters in their lineups. Over the years, you and I talked a lot about the controversial designated hitter (DH) rule, mainly because the American League employs one and the National League does not. It seemed reasonable to

us—allowing another hitter to bat for the pitcher, freeing up the latter to focus on pitching and to do what he does best. It seems necessary in some cases—not only in the game of baseball but in life too. When the Toronto DH came up to bat, I thought about all of the designated hitters who played a role in my life, allowing you and Dad to focus on the roles you played best: restauranteur and doctor.

Ella entered my life when I was a month old. You and Dad hired her to take care of the house and the kids while you both attended to your professions. She made my entire world go around. I think you would agree that, in many ways, Ella raised me.

When I started preschool, I couldn't wait to get home to Ella. Anticipating my arrival, she placed my blanket in the dryer, summoned Rabbie (my well-loved stuffed rabbit), and prepared my favorite grilled cheese. All three awaited me when I walked through the door. We sat side by side watching *The Jetsons* or *The Smurfs* while I clung to my Rabbie under the warm blanket and ate the sandwich she made me with a slab of butter and a tub of love.

On special days, we walked hand in hand to the National grocery store around the corner from our house—my tiny fingers locked in her gentle grip. I knew we were about halfway there when we came to the spot in the sidewalk where the tree roots caused it to buckle, forming a concrete mountain. She'd lift me up by one arm and swing me over it. "Safe and sound from the alligators!" I would announce to the neighbors.

In the back corner of the National, I stood on my tiptoes and reached up into the refrigerated case for my favorite snack—processed cheese and rectangular Club crackers housed in a two-compartment, plastic container. As soon as we paid, I ripped off the plastic and started spreading that fake yellow goodness all over the crackers before we even left the store. Often, I left a crumb trail behind me. (I suppose the abundant New Orleans roaches were happy about that, even if the manager wasn't.) I wouldn't get far before Ella told me to sit down: "There's no sense in walking and eating at the same time, Katie." My little legs dangled from the bench outside the store while I battled with the red plastic spreader, trying to scrape out every last ounce of fake cheese. Most of the time, the cheese stuck to the roof of my mouth. Unlodging it gave me something to do on our walk home.

I wanted to be exactly like Ella. Every day, I followed her around the house, copying the things she did. She taught me how to fold a perfect towel, the type of perfect fold you "see in the department stores," she proclaimed. And because of Ella, I knew the exact amount of Comet to use in the bathtub—enough to get all of the stains out of the grout but not too much that it went to waste. On days when her knees weren't bothering her, she would let me climb aboard her back so I could pretend to be a cowgirl, lassoing away.

And the best thing about Ella? Her hugs. She'd scoop you up in her large, pillow-like arms, making you feel like you could take a nap, you felt so safe.

Ella didn't have any kids herself, and I assumed she thought of me as her daughter. That's why I was so devastated the day she told me she had to leave. Her husband, Leo, wanted to move back to Mississippi to be closer to family. "But I thought we were family, Mom," I said to you as you tried to console me.

That was the last time you ever saw Ella.

A year after you died, and twenty-two years after my epic meltdown in that closet, I had dinner with a friend during which I told him all about Ella Mae. He probed me throughout dinner: "When was the last time you heard from her? What was her previous home address? How old would she be?" By the time we swallowed the last bite of our blueberry pie, he said, "We have to find her, Katie."

I *wanted* to find her. I tried many times over the years, to no avail. I sent letters to her home address and received them back with "return to sender" stamped in red. In college, I even wrote to Oprah, thinking she might connect us on one of her reunion shows. Nothing. Throughout, I wondered, *Does Ella want to find me?*

Not long after that dinner conversation, I received an email from my friend. *I think we found her,* he wrote. Right below those five words—five words I never thought I would see—Ella's current home address and telephone number appeared. I cried instantly, this time happy tears. I had waited decades to hear her voice; I didn't waste a minute rehearsing what I might say. I grabbed my cell phone and called her. Four rings and an answer:

"Hello?"

"Hello, Ella?"

"Who's this?"

"It's Katie. Katie Russell."

"*Katie?!* Is that you?"

"Yes."

"I don't believe it."

It *was* hard to believe. Ella and I had finally reconnected! A long conversation ensued during which she asked about each Russell family member. I told her you had passed away from cancer. She told me Leo, her husband, had died suddenly of a heart attack. She knew exactly how old I was and my birth date. When I asked her about the day she left, she said, "I hated to go." We caught up for over an hour, but I knew that wasn't enough time. I had a better understanding of the fragility of life after losing you, Mom. I wasn't going to lose another mother figure without making sure she knew exactly how I felt about her. I immediately made plans to visit Ella.

Off I went to McComb, Mississippi, by way of Baton Rouge. Driving my rental car down the winding Louisiana back roads lined with oak trees covered in dangling moss, the set of an old southern movie seemed to unfold outside my windows. It was all a bit eerie. I passed only one car and, besides Ella, no one knew my whereabouts. I didn't tell my family about my plans because I wanted to see her on my own. The solitude gave me time to process the magnitude of the moment. I wondered what Ella would look like after all these years. I wondered if she missed me. In hindsight, I recognized my parents paid Ella to take care of me. Did that mean she felt obligated to treat me like family? Did she think of me over the years as much as I had thought about her? Did she love me as much as I loved her? Most of all, I wanted to know this: Was she okay?

When I arrived, Ella opened the door and invited me into her warm embrace, then into her home. Suddenly, I was twelve again. Not only did I recognize the feeling of being in her loving arms, but she looked exactly the same. My first question was answered—Ella was okay.

We swapped stories at the Golden Corral (her favorite), peppering each other with questions and smiling about all the memories we shared. Before our collard greens and corn bread disappeared, I asked her how she felt about us. "Like family," she assured me.

I spent several hours with Ella that day, and I treasured every minute of reminiscing and reconnecting with her. Some days in your life you know you'll never forget, even as they're still unveiling themselves. My visit with Ella was one of those days.

A few weeks before you died, Mom, I remember lying next to you in bed while you cried—the same way I cried the day Ella moved. You weren't crying because you knew you were dying. You were sad for me because, as you said, "I don't want you to have to go through life without a mom."

I've thought a lot on that statement and the irony of it, since you often weren't present when I was a little kid. Did you know I missed you when you were away? Did you think about me when you were at work? I sometimes felt like you must have enjoyed being at the restaurant more than spending time with me. If how we spend our time reflects our priorities, your work took precedent over me, family, and pretty much everything else.

Could you have done a better job as a mom? Perhaps. Could you have done worse? Most definitely. Maybe all of those years when I thought you were too busy to be my mom, you were in the "dugout," ensuring I had the best person in my life to give me the best care possible. During my younger years, that person was Ella Mae. Because of you both, I've learned that when people leave—whether for a job or to a new city or to heaven—they don't stop loving you. Love is why they stay with you even after they're gone. How lucky I am to have had two moms who loved me and nurtured me in their own ways and whose love I carry with me each day.

Oh, and one other thing! I can't believe I almost forgot to tell you this. After lunch that day in Mississippi, Ella invited me back to her home. Atop a dresser, Ella had several family photos displayed. Wouldn't you know it? Prominently positioned next to the photographs of her blood relatives sat a family picture of us. It was tattered, worn at the edges, and sprinkled in dust. No doubt it had been there since the day she moved in.

For the entirety of my thirty-four years, I had considered Ella family. Now I knew Ella had considered us family too.

XO,

KATIE

8

BElong

MOM,

Since your death, I've often wondered why you loved baseball so much. While I inched closer to that answer with each ballpark visit, Miami unlocked a big clue.

I could have blindfolded you all the way to the game, lifted the red bandanna upon our arrival, and instantly, you would have known you stood in front of Marlins Park. Encircled by palm trees, the majestic structure—with its clean white lines framed by the bright blue sky—stood tall in the heart of the city. I discovered on my journey that, unlike other sports stadiums, modern-day ballparks often resemble the communities in which they reside. Only two miles from downtown, Marlins Park exemplified this in every way, both outside and inside. Welcome, a sign over the entrance gate announced. I knew, even then, it meant more than welcome to a baseball game. Welcome, fans, to the beautiful community of Miami!

Inside the ballpark, a retracting glass wall perfectly framed a view of the downtown skyline. Colorful mosaics reflected the city's diverse culture. In left field, the Clevelander brought a bit of South Beach to Little Havana. The bar showcased a swimming pool, some of Miami's hottest DJs, and its spirited libations.

Not far from the Clevelander, a sculpture rose in the area behind the left–center field fence. I didn't get to see it in action, because the Marlins never hit a dinger that day. The ostentatious seventy-foot-tall monument to everything Miami still left an impression. Mixed reviews aside (the sculpture has since been removed from the park), there's no denying the colorful and flashy display drew everyone's attention, even when not in motion. I'd seen it on television. Flamingos bounced. Marlins spun. Waves flowed back and forth. And birds soared—all while a fountain sprayed water into the air.

Don't worry—I still saw plenty of action, even without home runs. In between innings, dancers jumped onto the dugouts and grooved to Latin beats. Ushers wore brightly colored shirts as they shimmied to ballpark tunes, and concession vendors sported sunglasses (despite the roof being closed) as they zigzagged through the maze of seats.

The fans trickled in. Teenagers, smartphones in hand,

wore string bikinis partially hidden under their bandeau crop tops and cutoffs. Elders carried scorebooks, while kids held their parents' hands, skipping and pointing. Maybe you're a season ticket holder, or maybe it's your first game. It didn't matter. Baseball beckoned, and you came to be part of something. It's a club anyone can join.

I sat next to an exuberant couple who donned jerseys and Mardi Gras–like necklaces with plastic burgers and martinis strung between purple, gold, and green beads. Beers in hand, they photobombed most of my snapshots before leaning over and asking me to take a few of them. While they didn't know many players' names, any stats, or even some of the game's rules, I considered them fans all the same. I considered them in the club.

We high-fived when the Marlins recorded an out, and we danced in our seats and waved our hands, summoning a T-shirt. The familiar ballpark comradery allowed me to forget about everything else going on in my life. I forgot about the side effects of my cancer treatment; I forgot about what ballpark I planned to visit next; and I forgot about what time I needed to check in for my flight. By the seventh-inning stretch, we wrapped our arms around one another and swayed to "Take Me Out to the Ball Game."

I thought, *Yes, take me out to the ball game, where I can share in a collective moment of joy. Take me out to the ball game, where the political or ideological positions of people around me don't matter. Take me out to the ballgame, where my imagination and sense of wonder can run wild.*

Whether the ballpark packs in thirty-five thousand or comfortably seats five thousand, it contains communal energy. There's power when everyone feels connected to something bigger. And there's comfort in knowing that, even though you might have bills waiting or laundry stacked high, if only for a couple of hours, baseball is all that matters.

The sense of place and pace of baseball offered me the chance to connect to other fans while also leaving space for introspection. With each inning, I felt more attached to Miami's vibrant and beautiful culture and, at the same time, I felt more connected to you. It didn't matter that Miami lost that day. I won. I attended the Marlins game alone, but I never felt lonely.

Shortly after I completed my ballpark tour, I asked your friends why they thought you loved baseball. None of them knew the exact answer. However, one explanation stood out:

"Your mom loved Mrs. Gail Little, our high school English teacher. During the World Series, Mrs. Little canceled class and let us all listen to the baseball game on the radio. Your mom was really into it."

Of course you were.

Thinking about it takes me to your life in October 1956. I imagine you in your plaid uniform, sitting in a circle with

48

your friends all crowded around a radio. Bob Wolff's and Bob Neal's voices boomed, the bat cracked, and the fans roared, cheers echoing between the old southern mansion walls of Louise S. McGehee School.

You must have been starstruck by the big names playing that afternoon—Mickey Mantle, Yogi Berra, Jackie Robinson, Roy Campanella, among many other Hall of Famers. All the while, Faulkner and Twain listened in from the bookshelves surrounding you. Did you hang on the announcers' every word, wondering what would happen next? Or did you dream up your own scenarios? I don't think anyone would have predicted a perfect game. Did you?

Mrs. Little (and baseball) accomplished something big that day, something effective teachers do best: She created an opportunity for a student to tap into her imagination and dream big. At the same time, she made that student feel like she belonged to something larger than herself.

Isn't that what we all seek?

XO,
KATIE

49

9

BE Understanding

MAY 16

CINCINNATI REDS – GREAT AMERICAN BALL PARK

Hɪ Moᴍ,

Hundred-year-old oak trees blanketed our property on Seventh Street. I loved them. I remember one had a trunk so wide that it took two people's outstretched arms to hug it. And many hugs it deserved.

It dutifully provided shade on humid summer days when the thermometer repeatedly hit triple digits. And it was the prime hiding place during sibling water-balloon fights. When Rachel and I tired of riding our bikes, the tree became the perfect kickstand for my navy-blue, ten-speed Schwinn and her pink-and-white, banana-seat bike.

During October, that oak became the lynchpin to Benjie's Halloween antics. He tied clear fishing string around it and rigged a pulley system from the roof of our house, allowing him to open and close our front gate mysteriously as trick-or-treaters entered. In December, it glowed with white lights and two months later, during Mardi Gras season, a rainbow of beads adorned its branches. Come spring and toward the end of the school year, when the pranks ramped up, toilet paper enveloped it entirely.

No matter the time of year, that oak stood sturdy in the front of our home, with its branches wide open welcoming whatever came its way, good or bad.

One morning, Dad walked you, Rachel, and me to your car parked outside our house and right beside the oak tree. He opened the doors and tucked each of us into your station wagon. Once we were all in, he peered through the window, motioned with his finger, and advised, "Lock your doors."

You obliged, started the engine, and turned on the radio. "I'll be right back," you huffed when you figured out you'd forgotten your purse. As you left the car, it didn't take long to realize your purse wasn't the only thing that slipped your mind. The gear shift on the steering column pointed toward *D*. *D* for drive!

Immediately, the station wagon hopped the curb. Rachel screamed as the car started driving over the exposed roots and attempted to climb up the oak tree. Dad rushed over, jumped in with one foot planted on the pavement, and stretched his other leg into the car to firmly hit the brake. He reached inside and shut off the engine. The sudden jolt caused a piece of bark to dislodge from the tree, and a loud *crunch* echoed through the neighborhood as the car came to a rest. Dad shrugged his shoulders, gave an oops glance, and asked if we were all okay. We were. I wondered if the tree was okay. It was.

And if this story isn't evidence enough, Mom, I'll say it: you weren't a good driver. Airport runs stand out as among the worst/best examples. Merging onto I-10 felt like automobile roulette. I ended up white-knuckled and shrunk down in the back seat, waving to the angry driver who looked over at us as he passed. I became *really* good at the nonverbal sorry.

You preferred driving two-footed. As a result, your brake lights lit up the freeway despite there being no car in front of you. It occurred so frequently the person behind us could have easily thought you had your hazard lights on. (Now that I think about it, that might have been a good thing.) Brake. Accelerate. Brake. Accelerate. I'm nauseated even writing about it.

Whatever the reason, you couldn't seem to admit you were a bad driver, and it caused a ton of tension between us.

Considering your own driving misadventures, it's little wonder you were the best at forgiving all of your children for driving mistakes. At fifteen, newly licensed, I headed out to the lakefront where I noticed a major traffic backup. There appeared to be an accident or construction causing many cars to turn around. I naively followed the crowd right past a No U-turn sign. New Orleans police officers took note and pulled all of us over.

"Ma'am, you made an illegal turn back there."

"I'm really sorry. I thought there was an accident and

everyone was doing it—" He didn't even let me finish my sentence.

"Ma'am, if everyone jumped off the Mississippi River Bridge, would you do it?" I didn't have a response. Well, at least not one appropriate enough to say to a police officer.

He issued me a ticket.

I cried all the way home—scared and disappointed in myself. I told you the story and you extended your arms, raised your shoulders, and said, "Oh well, we all make mistakes." A hug followed.

Standing out in front of the Great American Ball Park before the game, I thought about us as I watched a juggler on stilts drop his baton right in the middle of his act. All around, fans stared. I cringed and looked up from my camera with concern, but he seemed unphased. He smiled and raised his arms and shoulders in an "oh well" gesture to his audience. He had already forgiven himself. Mistake embraced.

I wonder if things might have been different if you could have embraced your less-than-optimal driving skills. I certainly could have done a better job of embracing your shortcomings behind the wheel.

What if I could have been more like the juggler or the oak tree or you and Dad? Standing tall with open arms, no matter the situation or the season.

XO,
Katie

10

BE Resilient

MAY 29

HOUSTON ASTROS – MINUTE MAID PARK

OH MOM,

I wish you had been with me at this game in Houston, maybe more than most. I had so much I wanted to share with you. Before the action started, the majority of the fans were busy locating their seats, securing their favorite beverages and snacks, or waving their pen-holding hands while pressed against the back of dugouts in hopes of a coveted player autograph. I, on the other hand, focused on the jumbotron message and the pregame announcer alerting fans to the importance of hurricane safety. Ten years earlier, Hurricane Katrina became part of our story and part of Houston's as they housed thousands of evacuees from New Orleans. The announcement brought me back to the days during and after that deadly storm.

I'm not sure we ever really talked about what happened.

While Katrina swirled in the Gulf, your friends gathered for a neighborhood bridge game, one of your favorite activities. This time, however, you politely bowed out. In retrospect, you seemed to know something others didn't. At 3:00 a.m., you left our home in Pass Christian—alone, without telling anyone (Dad lived and worked in New Orleans during the week)—and hit the road. Something in your gut told you to go, and I'm proud you listened. You grabbed Zona, the dog; a pillow; and some utensils and turned your beat-up, gray SUV onto Highway 90 to head east. Had you not, the following day you would have been stuck in traffic with everyone else rushing to beat the storm or, worse, you might not have escaped at all. That intuition you modeled for much of your life, I now try to cultivate in my own life.

We lost so much in that storm. Gone were family photographs, over fifty years' worth of Christmas ornaments, my autographed picture of Andre Dawson, and the extensive collection of cookbooks you devoured over and over again. We nearly lost our minds while we waited to hear from Dad, who stayed behind to take care of patients in New Orleans with no air conditioning, no phones, no electricity, very little food, and only the clothes on his back. For more than a week, we didn't know whether or not he was alive. Yet, you never complained about losing your home or your things, including two-hundred-year-old heirlooms. Instead, in profound loss, you saw an opportunity to travel the country and see your kids.

Dad met you in Atlanta and you played endless Scrabble with Hugh and his wife, Christina. Then you flew to Washington, DC, to see Rachel and celebrated Dad's birthday at Rice, one of her favorite restaurants. While you stayed with her, Rachel even made you both answer a "get to know you" questionnaire she created. I think the loss of our childhood home made her want to hold on to her past and to her parents a little tighter. And when you came to San Antonio to visit me, Dad beautified my balcony with seasonal blooms while you and I watched playoff baseball. Spending time with you and Dad in those months after Katrina was an unexpected blessing. It will forever serve to remind me that there are gifts that reside in every moment, even the darkest ones.

The storm washed away so much, but we gained far more than what we lost. When the water receded, what remained were life's real treasures.

I don't think I'll ever forget returning home for the first time. Remember the black-and-white photograph of you on your wedding day, which somehow wound up on the other side of the neighbor's fence? We saw only a corner of it, sticking up out of the mud. Dad screamed when he unearthed it. I rushed over to him in time to see joy wash over his face as he admired your picture, tears in his eyes. Of all the photographs, that one survived? None of us realized then the photo would symbolize a positive shift about to happen in your relationship with Dad.

Shortly after the flashbulb popped to capture that scene on your wedding day, Dad began a career that meant most of his time was spent taking care of his patients. I've wondered how you managed to accept all of his late-night hospital rounds, the missed holidays, the school functions for six kids that you attended alone. Certainly not the life I envision for me and my future family. After Katrina caused the levees to break, completely flooding New Orleans, Dad suddenly had significant time away from work as the city began to rebuild. For the first time in your life, you had him all to yourself. Although you never told me, I sensed you longed for that. Who knew it would take losing everything to gain all you ever wanted?

Your remaining days numbered fewer than we had expected. Eight months later, we learned of your cancer diagnosis. Katrina forced you to find a new home in Alabama, where you spent your remaining years. This allowed us to preserve the memory of our childhood home as a happy place, not the place where your body and mind deteriorated as the cancer spread from your colon to your brain. Sure, our home in the Pass, the place that provided so much joy for so many, was gone. However, the overwhelming positive memory of the place remained intact. And four years after Katrina made landfall, we returned you to that place you loved so much, spreading your ashes among the wind and the water of Pass Christian, where your spirit now lives on forever.

And your spirit lives on in me too, Mom.

XO,
KATIE

11

BE Communicative

JUNE 5

COLORADO ROCKIES – COORS FIELD

Mom,

You knew better than anyone that Easter topped my list of favorite holidays. That is, until 2007.

My then boyfriend invited me to spend the holiday with him in Fort Worth. While I didn't want to miss the sibling sack races, Dad's Easter egg dyeing, and Peter Rabbit's appearance, I welcomed the opportunity to meet his family for the first time.

Easter morning, I awoke to a carefully curated basket filled with pastel treats, a beach towel, and a pool toy—the kind of basket you made for us as kids (and well into my twenties). He received major points for his reconnaissance work by calling Rachel to find out what I liked. And just like that, your traditions arrived in Texas.

Excited to tell you about my basket, a midmorning call home to wish you Happy Easter became less routine than expected. Instead of you or Dad, your six-year-old grandchild, Alexis, answered.

"Hi, Alexis! It's Aunt Katie. Happy Easter!"

"Hi, Aunt Katie."

"What are y'all doing?"

"Playing."

"Mabbie and Popsie playing with you?"

"No, Mabbie's in the hospital."

Seriously? How could you and Dad not tell me? Alexis knew and I didn't?

Soon after, I heard from Benjie that Dad had carried you to the car because you refused to go to the hospital. Too weak to put up a fight, you relented as Dad realized you needed more medical help than he could provide. We later learned a tumor in your colon nearly bled out. By the time I left Fort Worth and flew back to San Antonio a few days later, you had received an advanced colon cancer diagnosis.

⚾ ⚾ ⚾

For my eleventh ballpark, I met up with old friends from San Antonio to watch the Rockies take on the Marlins. The highlights? Giancarlo Stanton's 478-foot bomb demonstrated how much the altitude befriends hitters. And a torrential downpour caused a two-hour delay. Umbrellas of all sizes and colors sheltered fans as we tried to escape the rain-soaked night at Coors Field. Despite our best efforts, no one really avoided the storm, and the umbrellas didn't offer much protection once the hail began.

Your cancer diagnosis created its own hailstorm. Surgery and a partial removal of your colon didn't go well. An infection led to an extended hospital stay. Along the way, you developed a fistula and digestive issues.

Due to your dismal surgical experience, you decided to avoid traditional treatment and disregarded the doctor's plan. You chose to live on your own terms, taking a less-potent chemo pill while also maintaining your life as you knew it before the diagnosis. You traveled to New York and China. You gardened fiercely, read voraciously, and played your favorite games competitively. No one would have known you were suffering because you kept up your spirits.

For two years your body wrestled with the cancer, and I wrestled with understanding your reality and how I could help. Phone calls home went like this:

"How are you?"

"I am fine! Tell me about you."

"What did the doctor say? Is the cancer still progressing?"

"Things are great!"

Offers from me to visit you in New Orleans were flat-out rejected.

"No, you've got so much going on with your job. We've got everything we need. Your dad is taking great care of me. You don't worry about a thing. I'm fine!"

I knew you weren't fine. The thing is, Mom, no matter how much you told us *not* to worry, worrying was the only thing people who cared about you knew how to do. The lack of open communication only exacerbated our concerns. The storm persisted no matter the size of the proverbial umbrella or how aggressively you wielded it.

I wanted to weather the storm with you. I know you had good intentions, and you didn't want to burden us with your pain. And while I appreciated you trying to protect us, I struggled nonetheless.

I could have done a better job of asking the tough questions and addressing my own emotional needs as a caretaker. It didn't seem right, though, to focus on my needs while you suffered. Now, I better understand that the unexamined emotional tumors we hold in our bodies can be equally as damaging as the physical ones. I think we both neglected to realize that communication could have been the conduit for our healing. When you closed the door on your pain, I missed the chance to make sense of it.

The last time we ever spent together, Hugh, Charlotte, Benjie, Rachel, Dad, and I circled your nursing home bedside. We took turns telling you how much we appreciated and loved you. If there had been any doubt, we wanted to ensure you knew how we felt before you left this earth. Some days, I still ask myself why I waited so long.

You didn't respond to our love confessionals, and, frankly, you hadn't said anything all day that made any sense to us. Mumbles about your grandmother made it seem as if you hovered between two worlds.

At one point, Benjie leaned in and said, "Mom, it's okay to let go. We are all here. You can go."

Suddenly, a moment of clarity and exasperation. You opened your eyes, then your mouth:

"I'm trying!"

We looked at one another and smiled (and silently giggled a little) over your unexpected reaction.

Benjie's response, after collecting himself: "You don't *have* to go!"

We all knew you weren't going anywhere with all of us in the room. You wanted to be alone with Dad. So, we said our final goodbyes, packed up our things, and headed back to our respective homes.

On my flight to Austin, I considered the things that made you a person so many of us loved. Among these, your insistence on seeing where your kids lived every time one of us moved. Dorm rooms, apartments, houses—the actual place didn't matter. You wanted to *picture* us and our lives. I moved into my first home right before your passing. Despite your best efforts to convince Charlotte to bring you to Austin in your final weeks of life, you hadn't been well enough to fly.

You never saw my new home.

When I arrived in Austin, exhausted from more than my travels, I dropped my suitcase, closed my bedroom door, and crawled into bed. I squeezed KC, my stuffed dog, and prayed for your peace.

Not long after I fell asleep, I awoke to my bedroom door suddenly swinging wide open. Three hours later, my phone rang.

Dad delivered the news. I asked him what time you left.

But I already knew the answer.

And I knew more than that.

Thanks for opening the door, Mom.

XO,

KATIE

12

BE Compassionate

JUNE 6

ATLANTA BRAVES – TURNER FIELD

Hi Mom,

I've been asked many times why we became Chicago Cubs fans given that we lived in New Orleans. We could have easily been Braves fans. Atlanta-based TBS, like WGN, televised games nationwide, making both the Braves and the Cubs accessible to anyone who had cable television. Most of the time, I responded to inquiries about our love of the Cubs with, "My mom preferred an underdog." Thus, we were Cubs fans for life.

The Braves took the field as Hagan, Grace (two of your eleven grandchildren), and I found our seats in the outfield. Grace, her blonde hair pulled back in a messy ponytail like mine as a kid, took in the action with her pensive blue eyes. Reverence for the game appeared across her face as she held her first ever ballpark treat—Dippin' Dots. She didn't want to miss a thing. Was this how you felt watching

me as a child? The scene transported me back to my own childhood—watching baseball with you and eventually playing in my own games.

Carrollton Boosters, the local sports league, gave me my first start as a ballplayer—a first start that almost didn't happen. One day at school recess, I overheard my friends whispering about their impending tryouts and how nervous they were about getting selected for a certain team. A little investigative work on my part revealed we (or you, ahem) missed the league's application deadline. Shocker! You and Dad weren't good at those kinds of things. Thanks to Melissa's parents for making a phone call to the league and my above-average athletic ability, they found a spot for me on the Howard Weil team. My endangered softball career officially began.

I loved playing softball. I even loved *practicing* softball—the timed runs to first base, partner hitting against the fence, and, especially, batting-cage days. I loved the structure and predictability it provided for two hours every afternoon. The uniforms, however, left something to be desired. The exact opposite of my volleyball "bun huggers" that barely covered my tush, my softball uniform covered me head to toe in white and kelly green polyester. Talk about scratchy! And who could forget those fake stirrup socks, softball's most stylish fashion accessory?

Honestly, it didn't matter what my uniform looked like

or felt like. Game days were my favorite as I got to wear my jersey to class. That meant one less thing to think about in the morning when getting dressed. And, more importantly, it gave me a sense of pride walking through the halls as the boys would acknowledge me with a subtle, upward nod and offer their support: "Who y'all playing?" "What time does the game start?" "Go get 'em today!" I daydreamed through most of my classes, too excited about the game to focus on balancing equations or the lessons of Atticus Finch.

Your excitement may have exceeded even mine on game day. You rarely missed a game (impressive, given your busy schedule). Sometimes, you even drove for hours to watch me play in the small towns of rural Louisiana. No matter where we played, you were there. And most of the time, I liked having you there.

One game, in particular, stands out. A gorgeous spring day. No breeze, temperature in the upper seventies, the perfect conditions for a softball game. Per usual, you had arrived and found your seat before the ump yelled, "Play ball!" The team we played that day arrived late and seemed disheveled as they scurried off the bus and over to the field. They didn't have official uniforms. Instead, they wore mismatching shirts with markered-on numbers. Think *The Bad News Bears.*

By the start of the fourth inning, we led by double digits. I roamed my typical area in center field, particularly bored due to the lack of action. That is, until our pitcher gave up a walk. As the umpire pointed to first, letting the player know to "take the base," I heard loud clapping. This surprised me because the Bad News Bears didn't have any fans at the game that day. I looked over in the stands, and it appeared *you* were cheering as the hitter jogged to first. I thought, *Nah, it couldn't be.*

The next batter came up to the plate and squared around to bunt, attempting to move the runner to second. At this point, with their first and only base runner, their coach hoped to get on the board and prevent the dreaded bagel score. The hitter laid down a bunt, and, once again, I heard a loud clap. I glanced over at the stands while running to back up any throw that might come into second base. Sure enough, you had switched allegiances mid-game. No way I could have been mistaken twice.

After the game, I threw my equipment into the car and, before you could utter a word, said, "Moooom, what the heck were you doing cheering for the other team?"

"Katie, you were so far ahead. They didn't even have matching uniforms. Come on, lighten up, kid!"

I hated when you said to me, *"Come on, lighten up, kid!"* You preached this lesson often because you thought I took life too seriously.

I didn't understand your logic. Your daughter is playing for one team and you're rooting for the team playing against her? It made no sense. Somehow, your actions during that game stayed with me.

Back in Atlanta, I watched Grace's eyes take in the spectacle of baseball—the fans, the food, the festivities. I realized we weren't there to learn the rules of the game, or even to eat Dippin' Dots. We were there to learn the stories of the underdog.

The Atlanta Braves sported a losing record and played the role of the underdog against the visiting Pirates. Pittsburgh had already prevailed in the first game of the series and had won fourteen of its last sixteen games. In the bottom of the ninth and with the game tied 4–4, a rookie with zero career home runs stepped up to the plate. On the first pitch of the inning, he drilled a line drive over the right field wall. Atlanta earned the walk-off win. The underdogs came out on top!

All those years later, once again I heard you clapping.

XO,
KATIE

13

BE Adventurous

I WENT TO SEE A PSYCHIC MEDIUM, MOM.

My Volvo puttered down a neighborhood street in North Austin as I inched my way toward the unknown. I arrived early (no surprise to anyone who knows me), so I circled the block and pulled in front of another home. I turned off the car's engine and waited while my mind and heart raced.

Where am I? What am I doing? Oh, yeah, my trusted friend who'd lost her mother to cancer highly recommended I see this person. I didn't realize mediums live in the suburbs of Austin.

I'd begun to think about the afterlife more after watching you in your final days, seemingly between two worlds, talking to your relatives who were no longer alive. And I don't think I fully understood that night my door swung open. Maybe I wanted one more chance to talk to you. I'd heard about people who could communicate with the spirits of the dead, but I remained skeptical.

Perhaps I can blame television and film for overdramatizing the role of a spiritual guide. Scenes from *Ghost* with Whoopi Goldberg, in her long, golden robe surrounded by candles and a crystal ball, flashed through my mind. Somewhere between imagining the smell of incense and the sight of luminous rocks dangling from strings, I rang the doorbell.

"Welcome!"

Upon first glance, the home appeared to be like any other. A tan couch and a coffee bean–colored table sat on a cream tile floor. The neutral color palette matched her outfit—void of any brightly colored robes. As she escorted me into her office, I let out a deep breath, realizing I'd been holding it ever since the ding-dong.

After a brief introduction and prayer for protection, she began to call on her spiritual guides. Dubious, I continued to wonder how I'd ended up lying on a table allegedly surrounded by angels. And then she said:

"It's your mom. Did she cross over recently?"

I nodded, still skeptical and careful not to lead the witness.

"Hold on a minute. She's talking so fast. I can barely understand her."

The medium didn't finish her sentence before all my

skepticism flew right past the angels and out the window. Anyone who'd spent even five minutes with you knew you were the fastest talker east of the Mississippi River. Part enthusiasm, part southern drawl—with a dash of trademark quick-wittedness—you often left people wondering what in the heck you'd said. Already on to the next story, your listeners were still trying to make sense of the previous one. I needed no further evidence that somehow you were talking through the medium.

"She's telling me you never wanted to be like her. She says it's okay. She understands because she didn't want to be like her mom either."

True. I didn't. I spent my younger years wondering how we could be so different.

I believe we all have a splash of magic and a dash of logic that lives inside of us. As we grow older, the scale tips in one direction or the other, influenced by our life experiences and the people who surround us. You, Mom, overflowed with magic. I tipped toward logic.

Your magic translated into epic adventures as an adult. Hopping islands in Ireland. Safariing in Africa. Hiking the Great Wall of China. However, my favorite memories of you and your escapades transpired practically in our backyard.

After all, anyone can be adventurous when traveling. It takes something special to make sparks fly close to home.

As an early adopter of the New Orleans Jazz Fest, you dragged us along from the time we could walk. Our feet shuffled to keep up below the oversized festival T-shirts you'd purchased the year before, which now made for perfect dresses.

You exuded joy while eating crawfish étouffée and bobbing to a live soundtrack of the all-time great jazz musicians. Undoubtedly, this informal jazz education influenced me. I can't imagine many middle schoolers choosing Fats Domino, of all the musicians in the world, as I did for my class project.

Your love for festivals didn't end with music. You tried all sorts of persuasion tactics to get me to attend the Tennessee Williams Literary Festival with you, including promises of beignets and snowballs.

Whether by loading pillows and friends in the back of the pick-up truck for a mobile cocktail hour or by taking us on yet another trip to the bookstore, you had a way of turning the mundane into an adventure. How about my birthday, when you rode into the yard on a motorcycle, with Dad in a gorilla costume? Like ants scattering, I've never seen a group of kids flee an inflatable bounce castle so quickly. Half the kids screamed out of fear, and the other half shrieked out of happiness. Friends still mention that memory today.

Of all your adventures, I marveled the most at you opening a restaurant.

With six kids and zero formal training, you converted an old pharmacy into a restaurant named Gautreau's. I'd watched you for years on the back porch, cutting out recipes and ideas from magazines and storing them in binders. At a time when society believed a woman belonged in the home cooking, you became a female head chef of your own restaurant. While maybe not a logical decision, you had the guts to go out and do the thing you dreamed of doing. Ironically, this meant I sometimes ate chips and waffles for dinner, but I can't say I wasn't proud of you.

While you navigated life steered by an abundance of magic, my internal gauge barely registered any. I spent much of my childhood avoiding adventure. Perhaps my lack resulted directly from your overabundant spontaneity? Maybe your avoidance of planning forced me to be a planner? Regardless, I do know one thing. I certainly didn't lack a model for being adventurous or your encouragement in pursuing adventure, but my small attempts sometimes went awry.

One time I tried to perform a cherry drop, hanging by my knees from my bedroom closet rod. Due to space constraints, I didn't gain enough momentum to land on my feet and instead landed flat on my face and chest. The floor knocked the wind out of me. I thought I'd died in the closet while trying to emulate Mary Lou Retton.

I worried about death more than you knew. One time we were on the lakefront, watching Benjie's soccer game. You told me and my friend we could walk around as long as we didn't go near the street. Lured by the concessions that beckoned from the other side of the road, we decided to go on a mini adventure to load up our pockets with Pixy Stix. But we never made it.

As we stepped out onto the street, a car driving the wrong direction came to a screeching halt about a foot away from us. We turned around and ran back to you, high on emotions and low on sugar. I never told you that story. For much of my life, I lived with the secret and disturbing thought that I almost got my friend killed.

I harbored a lot of fear, which most likely thwarted my adventurous spirit. One night, I looked out my upstairs bedroom window and saw a burglar creeping along the perimeter of our yard. He held a gun in his right hand and kept turning his head to the right then the left, resembling a tennis match spectator.

Our house had been broken into so often I thought I might be jumping to conclusions. I yelled downstairs to Dad, "He's wearing a white T-shirt, so maybe I'm mistaken." Even my twelve-year-old brain knew you didn't wear a white T-shirt to rob someone at night. Since Rachel and you were asleep and the others weren't home, I decided to head down to be with Dad. "Don't come down here!" he yelled when he heard me on the stairwell. Frightened, I stopped in my tracks and took a seat. I remember peering through the wooden banister, shaking and begging Dad not to go out there and take matters into his own hands. Thankfully, he managed to scare him off from inside by banging on the windows.

I don't think I ever felt safe at home. And I'm pretty sure you and Dad never gave me the chance to talk about how I felt. I didn't know why I seemed more vigilant than my friends—always looking over my shoulder in crowds. And maybe my not feeling safe explains why I never slept soundly at night. I wonder if your overwhelming sense of adventure made me hesitant to tell you how I felt.

There are other stories too. Stories that have taken me years to process, through reading and therapy. Some that are yet to be discussed. Nonetheless, it's fair to say that during the years we spent together, I could have used a little more magic, and you might have benefited from a little more logic.

Something had changed in me, though, by the time I entered Busch Stadium—my thirteenth ballpark in two months. I hate to admit this, given the Cardinals' status as the longtime nemesis to our Cubs, but the downtown ballpark—with the iconic arch framing the outfield and our familiar Mississippi River a few blocks away—left an impression.

This baseball adventure marked the most spontaneous and fearless thing I'd ever done in my life. As it turns out, it's also the thing that brought me the greatest joy. While sitting in the stands, unflappable in the rain, I could feel my internal magic meter rising. *Who needs dry clothes anyway?*

That day I visited the medium, you said it was okay not to be like you. But maybe I'm a little more like you than we realized—one of the many things I've learned by stepping into America's ballparks.

XO,
KATIE

14

BE Mindful

DEAR MOM,

The lines to get into Target Field wrapped around the ballpark. While it's possible the sunny, seventy-five-degree summer day had something to do with it, the blame more likely belonged to the new security measures put in place at the start of the season. Screenings at all thirty stadiums now consisted of mandatory metal detectors, which increased wait times to enter. Target Field won't be remembered as the ballpark with the shortest line, but I will remember it for what transpired while waiting in that line.

Excited about visiting my fourteenth ballpark, in a state I'd never visited before, I joined other eager fans in the middle line. Bumping shoulders, stepping on the backs of heels, and smelling both sweet floral scents and not-so-appetizing aromas are all inevitable in crowds. But a whack on my calf? That wasn't something I'd ever experienced

until that day. I turned around and saw two visually impaired young men standing behind me, one with a white cane that grazed the ground and my leg.

I introduced myself, and we chatted a bit about baseball. I told them when the line moved and how far we still had to go until we arrived at the ballpark's pearly gates. At one point, I called out the youngest man's name as he veered into another line. Their ability to navigate entry into a ball game astonished me.

Twenty minutes later, I said goodbye to them as I began walking through the metal detector. The experience stayed with me. *How would they find their seats or top their hot dog with the perfect ratio of mustard and relish?* I waited nearby to see if they made it through okay and grabbed my camera from my purse. I wanted a photograph to remind me of the moment and the crossing of our paths.

🂠 🂠 🂠

Imagination is a gift we've all been given, and our capacity to grow it comes with practice. I'd learned to expand mine by meditating, reading about others' experiences, and being more mindful. That day, I imagined what it would be like to attend a baseball game without eyesight.

With my eyes closed, I could hear the park's vibrations. The sound of fans' shoes pounding the pavement, the snap of the ball hitting the catcher's mitt, and the pop of peanuts being freed from their shells. I knew when a fan nearby left his seat, as the squeak of a loose screw announced his departure long before the perfunctory, "Excuse me." The salty smell of bratwurst and popcorn hinted at enough of a sodium bomb to keep me from purchasing either. And I didn't need to look to know that a fan in the row behind me gobbled up nachos. My clue? The double crunch followed by a slurp.

Then, with opened eyes, I noticed the sweat beads on the beer vendor's face, which originated from his forehead, below the brim of his Twins cap. The droplets trickled down his cheeks, landing on his bright yellow shirt and disappearing into his polyester collar. I began to listen more deeply to those around me. And thank goodness I did, or I might have missed out on meeting Tammy.

Tammy, a local sitting next to me, attended the game with her family. We talked about our lives, why we loved baseball so much, and our playoff predictions. She exuded a nurturing persona, with her soft-spoken questions and attentiveness to my answers. Mom, it almost felt like you were speaking through her. Somehow, I felt understood by a total stranger.

A few innings later, I began to feel overheated, despite being in shorts and a short-sleeved shirt. A bit worn down from all the traveling, I decided to leave the game early and head back to the hotel to rest. I didn't leave without handing Tammy my card, a gesture that would lead us to a long-term pen-pal relationship.

At the hotel, I took my temperature. Yes, I carry a thermometer with me when I travel because of chemotherapy and my oncologist telling me at every appointment, "If you get a fever above 100.5 degrees, don't take any medicine. We don't want to mask it. Instead, call my office." The thermometer beeped, and I panicked when I pulled it out of my mouth and saw 102 on the display.

I called my ob-gyn's office because his nurse had left me a message earlier in the day, asking me to return her call. Turns out the urine sample I'd provided for my annual appointment (the day before I left for my trip) indicated I had a significant urinary tract infection, and I needed an antibiotic.

I dragged myself back out onto the streets of Minneapolis and to the drug store. My eyes began to water and my head began to hurt—more so from the anxiety than from the infection. It felt scary to be in a new city alone and sick for the first time since my chemo treatment ended. My heart raced, and I wondered if something was seriously wrong with me.

That vulnerability, while clearly not on the same level as losing one's sight, gave me a glimpse into what it must feel like for those two young men I'd met in line at the game, making their way in an unfamiliar place.

I realized that flying to Missouri the next day, while sick, might not be the best idea. I needed to alter my ballpark plans, the first hiccup in the journey. I called my friend Angie and delivered the bad news that I wouldn't be seeing her and the Kansas City Royals when we'd originally planned. Of course she understood, but I felt awful. I hated letting people down. Historically, this mindset often led me to do things I had no interest in doing. But I'd learned to take better care of myself after treatment. I rebooked my flight so I could fly home the next day.

My mind spinning, I turned on the television. I settled, unsurprisingly, on highlights of the Twins game.

Darn it, Mom! I missed the dramatic ending. The Twins had struggled at the plate as of late. Kennys Vargas sat at the top of the slump list, but late in the game, he broke through. In the bottom of the ninth, he hit a solo shot with two outs, lifting his team to a 2–1 victory—a walk-off home run! Slumps are meant to be broken, and I knew I'd be back at a ballpark in no time.

While struggling to fall asleep, I lay in bed cocooned in sweaty sheets caused by my body's attempt to break the fever. I opened my laptop and downloaded photos from my camera. Next to me Mac (my travel, stuffed doggie) and a room service tray with a big bottle of water, a peanut butter sandwich, and a rainbow of fruit to keep me company.

Sorting through over a hundred photos from the game, I came across a thumbnail of the photograph I'd taken of the young men behind me in line. I clicked to enlarge it, realizing immediately the image was out of focus—the only blurry shot from the day. Bummed at first, I soon recognized its significance and the irony.

While the photograph won't win any awards, it stands apart from the others I snapped that day—a reminder of a baseball game experienced through their eyes. And a reminder that a photograph has the power to bring us back to a particular place and time. This one will forever transport me to the day two young men in Minnesota changed the way I see baseball. The day that I became more mindful of the moments in and around the ballpark.

After all, isn't that why I'm on this journey, Mom?

XO,

KATIE

15

BE Ready

JUNE 29

BALTIMORE ORIOLES – ORIOLE

PARK AT CAMDEN YARDS

Mom,

No doubt you would have shared my enthusiasm for arriving early to the Orioles game. I'm surprised more people don't do the same. Pregame batting practice provides a behind-the-scenes, up-close-and-personal look at players and their routines. VIP experience without the VIP costs. Sometimes practice gets a bad rap. Many think it's boring because there's no competition. Sure, there's no winning in practice. Yet, without practice, there *is* no winning.

Do you remember me constantly practicing basketball when I was little? Dad installed a hoop in our yard at home in New Orleans and also in Pass Christian. This gave me endless opportunities to play HORSE (or PIG, a shorter version for those less enthused about playing with me). I could count on Ella at least twice a week. But most of the time, I shot hoops by myself. Even at night, you could find me lying in bed, aiming that squishy, orange ball in the direction of the Nerf net secured over the door. Rachel would retrieve for a little while, but only if I promised her she could use my Garfield phone to call her friends.

I spent many summer days in Pass Christian shooting baskets. Benjie entertained my hoops obsession more than most in the family. He even taught me a few things, including his famous behind-the-back bank shot. After best three out of five, when we were good and hot, we'd sprint to the pool, Benjie yelling, "Last one's a rotten egg." Not surprisingly, I trailed him, but with the perfect reply: "First one's got to eat it."

After a few rounds of Marco Polo and motorboat, we began shooting hoops again. This time, in the pool while treading water. That's when the floating, blue-and-white basketball goal came in handy. It also aggravated you most, Mom, while you attempted to swim laps. I'd convinced Dad to buy it at Walmart one day when we went to buy you more Cokes. Walmart trips with Dad were the best. We usually came back with some new toy. "Russ! You were *only* supposed to get Cokes and the *Sun Herald*!" The ultimate yes-man, Dad couldn't help himself.

All of the hours practicing basketball in the yard, from my bed, and in the pool, meant Katie Russell was ready to be part of a team. I knew it. You knew it. Problem was, New Orleans had no girls' basketball leagues. "Well, then, you'll join the boys' league," you assured me. That seemed impossible to me, but you insisted. Dad didn't like the idea. "Anne, she can't do that." He didn't question my ability. He questioned whether it would be safe. He didn't want to see me hurt—emotionally or physically. At that time, a distinct gender line existed in youth sports, and crossing it wasn't the norm.

Norms weren't really your thing, gender or otherwise. Your older brother, Tommy, who lived in the apartment above your restaurant, shared Dad's skepticism. And your oldest son, Hugh, worried about me too. He reminded you that you wouldn't let him play baseball because you didn't want him to hurt his arm, making him the only one of his friends who didn't get to participate. (He *still* has *all* sorts of feelings about that.)

Not sure how we convinced Dad (or if we ever did), but Hugh and Tommy cast aside their doubts and decided if I was going to do this, they wouldn't let me do it alone. You had to work, so the three of us walked down Danneel Street, from Gautreau's to Newman School, me sandwiched between Hugh and Tommy, my bodyguards.

There's no mistaking the sounds of a gymnasium—a concert of squeaky sneakers mixed with the percussion of the ball pounding the wooden floor. I could still hear the thumping of my heart despite the noise. *Maybe this is not the best idea.* As I second-guessed our decision, I spotted my friend Abbie among the sea of sweaty boys. Turns out one other parent had the same idea. Phew! There were two of us. My shoulders relaxed a little, and my heartbeat began to slow.

I didn't play like Larry Bird that day. But I wasn't the worst player in the gym either. I made a team! Well, let's be honest—everyone makes a team in elementary school.

That season, the league held all practices and games in Tuohy Gymnasium—the gym best known for its namesake, the Tuohy family, which Michael Lewis portrayed in the popular book and movie *The Blind Side*. It seems fitting that would be the place where I learned looks can be deceiving, and with a lot of practice and the support of someone who believes in you (thanks, Mom), you can do anything.

Long before Mo'ne Davis graced the cover of *Sports Illustrated* and landed in the hearts of all who watched her stellar performance on the mound at the 2014 Little League World Series, there was Katie Russell. Tuohy Gymnasium. And the very last game of the season.

While I sat on the bench most of that game, late in the action I traded riding the pine for jogging the maple. Any minor scouting done by the other team would have revealed to the coaches that they didn't need to guard me. The ball wouldn't be coming my way even with Hugh yelling, "Throw it to the girl!" I had no stats despite having attended every game.

With the clock winding down and my teammate trapped, I threw up my hands to let him know I was open. In a blink, I had the leather "rock" in my hands for the first time all season. No one had ever passed me the ball in a game. Without hesitation, I drove the lane and elevated for a layup. I'd done it thousands of times in my backyard and watched enough NBA games to know exactly how it looked.

It didn't go the way I envisioned.

Instead, a boy from the other team charged at me.

Knocked off-balance, I landed awkwardly on the court. (I think I heard you gasp from the bleachers.) And the ball landed nowhere near the goal. The dad volunteer referee blew the whistle and, with that, I had a date with the free-throw line.

I toed the stripe. I had no helmet to hide my face. No softball stirrup socks to cover my trembling legs. This was my one shot (or two). I dribbled the ball three times, took a deep breath, bent my knees, kept my elbow in, eyed my target, and followed through. On that night, in a sweaty Uptown New Orleans gym, I was the outlier. In more ways than one. I made both shots. Nothing but net. Swish. Swish.

I don't think we ever know when we get our shot. That's the beauty and tragedy of life. You keep practicing, and when the opportunity presents itself, you're ready. I can't help but think about how your cancer journey occurred only a few years before mine. I guess the universe gave me the opportunity to practice navigating cancer before facing the ultimate battle myself.

Thanks to you, that practice helped me beat the greatest opponent of my life.

XO,
KATIE

16

BE Happy

JULY 4

BOSTON RED SOX – FENWAY PARK

Namaste Mom,

Did you ever consider attending a meditation retreat when you were alive? For me, the amazing thing about them is how calm and balanced I feel after I attend one. I'd found them to be the antidote to my anxiety and, thus, began to attend them as often as I could. During the retreat, the sage, cross-legged teacher inevitably asks us to close our eyes and mentally travel to our happy place. "Go to the place that brings you joy, the place where you dwell in peace."

Instantly, I'm transported to the back seat of our station wagon, the straps of my blue-and-green tankini carefully tucked underneath my hand-me-down dress. My new jelly shoes rested atop my Strawberry Shortcake suitcase, filled with nothing more than my summer uniform: T-shirts, bathing suits, and neon Umbro shorts. After the click of my lap belt, we drove east toward the Gulf of Mexico, to the oak-lined streets of my summers, to Pass Christian—my happy place.

If that same teacher inquired about the location of America's happy place, I suspect many would answer Fenway Park. With all apologies to Wrigley Field, Fenway is America's ballpark. For more than one hundred years, the oldest ballpark in Major League Baseball has resided in the hearts and minds of all who love the game, despite allegiances to other teams.

What better day to experience America's ballpark than America's birthday? My friend, Kate, and I donned head-to-toe red, white, and blue and headed down Brookline Avenue. The Green Monster, baseball's most famous out-field wall, awaited our arrival.

Turns out, the left-field wall dressed for the occasion as well. A gigantic American flag draped across it, creating the perfect patriotic backdrop to the national anthem and a row of service members in military salute. I always get choked up during the anthem, but this time felt particularly meaningful as we acknowledged the holiday's significance.

A couple sitting in front of us wore his-and-hers bedaz-zled flag hats. Below her sequined cap dangled renowned second baseman Dustin Pedroia's face—framed in the form of earrings. You would have been enamored by the couple's festive look and, no doubt, you three would have left the stadium as best friends.

The holiday spirit didn't end with the fans. Boston's mascot, Wally (the green monster the kids come to see), delighted fans both old and young. The vendors brought their A game too. They roamed the concrete walkways, carrying heavy loads while simultaneously fueling the stomachs of Fenway's faithful. They sported highlighter-yellow caps and shirts so as not to be missed, but that's not what made them stand out.

One launched peanuts five rows up, hitting his target on the first try. Another managed to balance his beer tray on a knee while pouring a cold one and collecting money from a thirsty patron twenty heads down. And the purveyor of Fenway franks, with a magician's sleight of hand, prepared a link right before my eyes, faster than I could ask, "How much?"

At one point in the game, the crowd began the wave. As I looked right to gauge the timing for our section, I noticed the picture-perfect scene and grabbed my camera. A beach ball hovered, fingers danced in the air, and fans flopped back into their seats. In the center of my shot, an everyday Superman walked through the crowd and contributed to the wave while double-fisting beers—a nod to all the superhero drinkers throughout the ballpark that day.

If a cape were to be worn in our family, it definitely belonged to you, Mom (aka Superwoman), especially in Pass Christian.

You choreographed our summers with ease and enthusiasm, somehow keeping six kids and countless friends entertained and happy for weeks on end. We swam from sunup to sundown, rode bikes to the local snowball stand, and, with greasy fried shrimp po'boy hands, we laid Scrabble tiles by the pool.

When I needed a break from the sun, or from Rachel's endless requests to play Yahtzee, I'd go to my bunk bed and snuggle into the red, white, and blue striped sheets to read my Berenstain Bears book. A nearby train would blow its horn and shake the house, adding a bit of nostalgia to the reading adventure. I'd pause right before Mama Bear delivered the moral lesson to Brother Bear and Sister Bear, wondering if any of my siblings had placed pennies on the tracks—unbeknownst to you and Dad—and would soon return with a flattened piece of copper.

If summers in Pass Christian were my happy place, the Fourth of July stood out as the happiest day of them all.

Independence Day began when you issued our annual holiday T-shirt. Whether iron-on transfers, puffy paint, or even professionally made, you personalized our shirts by birth order—five stars for me, the fifth child. Little time passed before those shirts landed in the grass as we peeled them off and jumped into the pool.

We'd begin to play water games, including my favorite, sharks and minnows. Every now and then, a waft of barbecue grilled chicken floated past my minnow nostrils as I came up for air after safely dodging the shark.

At some point, we'd break from swimming to eat sour cream and onion Lay's, washed down with a bottle of Barq's root beer. Next, we walked barefoot (more like tiptoed) across the steaming asphalt to our neighbors for our annual cabbage ball match. After about five innings, the adults, whose beverages had run dry, began daydreaming of refills, and we headed back to our house—just in time to eat some of Hugh's delicious barbecue and the homemade flag cake we'd baked with our cousins.

Not surprisingly, the day ended with fireworks. Neighbors up and down Highway 90 came to sit on the seawall in front of our house. Dad notoriously overspent at the fireworks tent. And who could forget the year Benjie dug a nine-foot circle in the sand, about four feet deep? Inside, he'd carved out benches for us to sit on and a table in the center on which to place our drinks. Made entirely of sand, the '84 fireworks bunker remains a point of family pride to this day.

I'm not sure Benjie was convinced the idea would work, as he dipped the wooden-handled shovel in the sand and dug his first scoop. But you knew the project would be worthwhile either way. You encouraged us to explore and try new things, no matter the outcome. Benjie beamed and you sat encircled by family and friends, smiling and laughing as the seagulls sang their last song of the day. With a cocktail in one hand, you leaned back against the sand wall and tossed your hair to the side, and I saw your face light up under the first fireworks. Pure happiness!

Later that week, we often boiled crabs. In the early morning, you and Benjie waded out to the channel markers, carrying vinyl-coated wire traps filled with chicken-neck bait. A milk jug masquerading as a buoy dangled as you walked the hundred yards from our house to the beach. The next day, you'd retrieve the traps.

If the tide cooperated, sometimes you'd let me tag along. I'd get the first attempt to pull the trap out of the brackish water. On days when its weight overwhelmed me, Benjie came to the rescue. We watched his swole biceps. "Woah, this has to be the most we've ever caught!" And then, to our surprise, the trap would be filled with a few crabs—and a big ol' wad of seaweed weighing it down. We'd laugh, imagining the crabs and seaweed conspiring against us. Turns out crabs use seaweed to hide from predators, and not only on the seafloor.

For lunch, you boiled the crabs while the kids were supposed to set the table underneath the stilt house. In between placing the napkins and utensils on the wooden picnic table, I'd challenge someone to a Ping-Pong match. Miraculously, by game point, the table stood transformed (thanks, Dad) and ready for you to dump the medley of crabs, potatoes, and corn on the *Sun Herald* tablecloths. John Denver played in the background, while the smell of Hawaiian Tropic sunscreen, pool chlorine, and tractor gasoline from the garage behind us lingered.

Always resourceful, we used the backsides of our knives as makeshift crab mallets. In between smashing and picking, we planned the afternoon's activities and debated who we thought would win Wimbledon. At some point, we'd raise our gooey crab hands to indicate who was in for a croquet match or the next round of hearts, flinging crab and gulf juice all over one another and the concrete floor. Everyone around the table laughed and continued stuffing their faces. No doubt in my mind, Pass Christian was everyone's happy place.

On August 18, 2009, Benjie waded out to the channel marker with you one final time. Instead of a crab trap, he carried a bronze urn that held your ashes.

We made sure you are forever in our happy place, Mom.

XO,
KATIE

17

BEcome

DEAR MOM,

My Uber driver dropped me at the foot of the Roberto Clemente Bridge near PNC Park for the Pittsburgh Pirates game. The suspension bridge closed to vehicular traffic during game days. Decked out in Pirates gear, pedestrians of all ages took advantage. The overpass also dressed in support of the local team—painted a shade somewhere between traditional yellow mustard and its fancier French cousin, Dijon.

My Converse and I stepped onto the bridge and into the excitement. We didn't get far, though, stopping every two feet to take photographs. Kids peeked under the railing and through the steel grate to see the party boats and Jet Skiers passing underneath. White tents strung along the southbound lane displayed local artists' crafts for sale. Locks of all shapes, painted with hearts and couples' names and monumental dates, decorated the side of the bridge. Every

so often a lamppost with potted pink flowers dangled from above. The hub of action provided the perfect subjects for my camera lens, but it didn't take long to realize the prize-winning shot was PNC Park.

Sitting on the banks of the Allegheny River, the ballpark appeared to rise out of the water. Boats dropped people off for the game at a dock situated right in front of giant, navy-blue-and-white letters: *P*, *N*, and *C*. The view from the bridge revealed the ballpark's unique two decks of navy-blue seats, rather than the typical three decks seen in most MLB ballparks. The lack of center field stands allowed for a full view inside for any passerby—in other parks, a glory available only to ticketholders.

Even with the great people watching and the gorgeous view of PNC, the bridge's namesake didn't escape my attention. After all, Roberto Clemente was one of the greatest baseball players of all time and the first Latin American inducted into the National Baseball Hall of Fame. His off-field contributions made him even more worthy of the many awards he received, both during his lifetime and posthumously. He held free baseball clinics for kids from low-income families, and he provided financial aid to people in his native Puerto Rico. In 1973, MLB renamed the Commissioner's Award to the Roberto Clemente Award, to honor one player annually who demonstrated Clemente's commitment to community involvement.

I assumed the walk to the game would be the highlight of the day and, once inside the ballpark, it would be baseball as usual. I'd soon discover, I'd been wrong. Upon entering the gate, I ignored the salty smell of hot dogs luring hungry patrons and headed straight to the top row. Along the way, I dodged several kids zigzagging through seats, many still energized from their Fourth of July festivities a day earlier. Eventually, I reached the summit, pirouetted to take in the view, and stood breathless (not from the long climb).

The downtown skyline, river, bridge, and baseball diamond created a beautiful urban mosaic. Pittsburgh showed off from every angle. I now knew why travel and baseball websites consistently rated the ballpark as one of MLB's best.

After my trip, I learned Rachel had studied the building of PNC Park during her time as a master's student in city and regional planning at the University of North Carolina at Chapel Hill. It served as a case study on how to finance controversial city projects. Tom Murphy, Pittsburgh's mayor at the time the stadium was built, inherited a city in economic distress, and the idea of building a new ballpark didn't sit well with taxpayers. The struggle to finance the ballpark struck out with voters, and the deal failed numerous times. Despite the resistance, Murphy persisted, eventually finding a way to fund it. Now, PNC Park is a crucial city landmark and a point of civic pride.

The former mayor visited Rachel's class to provide a

firsthand account. His lesson for the day? As a city planner, your role is to have the vision to see what something
might become. Even amid resistance or when it makes you
unpopular, at times the fortitude and persistence pays off.

While I wasn't aware of it at age thirteen, you included
the mayor's sentiment in your lessons for me. For example,
you insisted that, if I received an invitation for an event, I'd
be required to go. I resisted this on many occasions, often
silently. While my words didn't convey my dissatisfaction,
my face often did.

Entry to the teenage years brought abundant invitations and a crowded social calendar. At thirteen, many of
my Jewish friends celebrated their bar/bat mitzvahs. Each
celebration consisted of a service during the day, followed
by an elaborate party later that night. Most of my classmates
attended only the fancy party, typically hosted in a hotel ball-
room. That's not how things worked in our family. "If you
want to go to the party, you go to the service," you'd tell me.

You dropped me off on the curb of St. Charles Avenue,
in front of the synagogue. Annoyed you made me go alone, I
slammed the car door while you were still talking. I walked
in and found a seat in the back corner. I watched as people
entered, wondering about the rules for covering your head
and why it seemed like all the other kids my age had a parent with them. Where were you?

When the service began, I hung my head and awkwardly

mouthed words I didn't understand. As the chanting increased, I zoned out. Sometime between dreaming about king cake and beating my opponent in soccer that week, the service ended and I scurried to the door, trying to exit before anyone noticed me. The conversation in the car usually went like this:

"How was it?"

"It was fine."

Neither of us would mention the topic again. Until the next one.

⚾ ⚾ ⚾

At the age of thirty-eight, Roberto Clemente died in a plane crash while on a mission to deliver aid to earthquake victims in Nicaragua. That's what he did. He showed up for people. He showed up for his teammates, on and off the field.

That's what you taught me. You show up for people—for their big life events or when tragedy strikes or just because.

I became that person you coached me to be, Mom. I strive to be someone who shows up for my friends and family. How could I not? You ensured I had a lot of practice. I resisted it, much like the people of Pittsburgh did in building PNC Park.

But sometimes, the things we resist become the things we cherish most.

XO,

KATIE

18

BEhind the Scenes

JULY 7

WASHINGTON NATIONALS – NATIONALS PARK

110

HEY MOM,

Well, it was a tough day for the Nationals. No action at the plate in this shutout game, but the action behind the scenes more than made up for it!

My friend Steph, who works for the Nationals, invited me to the ballpark a couple of hours before the team played the Cincinnati Reds. If being at batting practice in Baltimore felt special, this exceeded even *my* baseball imagination.

I tiptoed through the bullpen. I peered into the dugout. I eavesdropped on the ushers having their pregame meeting in the seats, and I watched political-pun-named vendors prepping food. The fine folks at Senators Sausage grilled links. The dedicated employees of Steak of the Union chopped onions. Ever seen a ball of pretzel dough twisted and transformed into a giant W? Impressive! With the District Brews' kegs tapped, popcorn popped, and Bullpen burritos about to be wrapped, my excitement overflowed.

And that wasn't even the best part! Want to know the highlight of arriving at a ballpark before the gates open?

Sitting in the stands with no other fans in sight.

I immersed myself in a sea of empty blue seats. Each one begged for a human to sit and shield it from the hot summer sun. Freshly cut grass perfumed the air. Snow-white bases awaited their first dirt-caked footprint. The batter's box chalk lines hadn't yet made an appearance.

Enveloped in the stillness, thoughts of you and behind-the-scenes memories at your restaurant flooded my mind.

Like preparing for a baseball game, running a restaurant isn't glitz and glamour, despite what patrons might think. For me, both of your restaurants, Gautreau's and Absolute Bar & Grill, taught me many lessons. I grew up among our family of employees, behind the scenes.

Not even a teenager and barely tall enough to see over the counter, I stood on my tippy-toes in my Wigwam socks and Reebok high tops in Gautreau's kitchen, signing checks for produce deliveries. "Place the lettuce over there, Bryan." I mastered your Anne A. Russell signature—big loop for the first *A*, medium loop for the second *A*, and a barely visible last name where the *e* and *ll*'s looked identical. (I'd have been a perfect forger if I ever needed to sign your name on a bad report card, but thankfully I never got one!)

I answered the phones for reservations while you prepped for the night with the chef de cuisine, Armand. I loved the game of piecing together the reservation puzzle. A regular would call last minute and want table three with Bomba as the waiter. A party of four wanted to become a table of five. "Can we move our reservation time up thirty minutes?" As a boutique restaurant, there were few tables, and botching one reservation could cause an entire evening to collapse before the night even started. From this experience, I learned my first lesson on telling people no. (Thirty years later, I'm still working on that.)

Between calls, I crawled on my hands and knees, placing pink Sweet'N Low packets underneath table legs to balance them. I folded napkins, polished the brass on the front door railing, and filled the salt and pepper shakers. I hated when I rushed and spilled, forcing me to retrieve the broom from the creepy cleaning closet.

On special days, you asked me to prepare the snow peas for the night's dinner. Robert (the dishwasher) and I sat across from each other on crates, snapping off one end of the pea, pulling out the string that linked that end of the snow pea to the other end. Then, with a flourish, snapping off the other side.

During the snap-pull-snap, we talked about sports. And when our fingers grew tired, we'd put our sports talk into action. I'd jump up, and he'd send me long—all the way down the alley to the gate—and toss me the football. Robert's cornrows bounced against his neck as he stepped back in the makeshift pocket, between the defensive tackles (aka trash cans), and let the ball fly. We probably threw longer than you wanted, but not long enough for me. I could have played football in the alley with Robert all day, even with the less-than-desirable odor of last night's meals lingering.

At Absolute Bar & Grill, a more casual pub, I completed my homework at the bar, asking Eddie B. to check my math calculations in between his cocktail crafting. All correct meant a hit from the soda gun. What kid wouldn't do their homework for endless Shirley Temples? He'd add more than one cherry, if I were lucky. Not long ago, I saw him bartending at Pascal's Manale. Same red vest. Same big blue eyes. Only thing different? Not much hair left!

Michael, another bartender friend, steered clear of homework help. While you worked, we passed the afternoon hours with magic tricks. My favorite? Turning an ordinary one-dollar bill into a dashing bow tie. I've performed it hundreds of times since and still do it to this day when I'm stuck somewhere and in need of a crowd pleaser. It never fails to elicit laughs and at least one "Show me how to do that!"

I loved those guys—Robert, Eddie B., Michael, and many others. So much so, I missed them every summer when I spent a month at Rockbrook Camp. While other girls penned letters to their parents, I lay in my bunk in Half-Pint cabin and wrote to the restaurant employees. Coming home from camp to see my letter stuck on the refrigerator at Absolute meant they must have missed me too, right?

I learned to think of people in the restaurant like family by watching you, Mom. You often showed up for them outside of the restaurant, attending funerals and weddings for their close family members. And you had plenty of your own behind-the-scenes experiences, didn't you? Working long hours, managing employee schedules and emotions, and punching numbers on the calculator. Despite the fact the restaurant consumed you, which meant less time with me, I recall those days fondly.

Seeing the bustling hours before the game in DC reminded me of those behind-the-scenes days. I made sure to thank everyone from the ticket scanner to the bathroom attendant. I wanted to acknowledge the work and magic they put into the baseball game didn't go unnoticed by me.

While their names may never see the bright lights, the pretzels never take shape, the peas never snap, and the tables never get balanced without everything and everyone involved in those quiet moments, behind the scenes.

XO,

KATIE

19

BE Strong

JULY 8

NEW YORK YANKEES – YANKEE STADIUM

Oн Mom,

Everything is blurry and the beeping constant. The doctors have cut my neck open, collected what they needed, and sewn me back up. Someone is telling me to sit up, but I can't seem to lift my arms or legs. I drift in and out, enveloped in a haze—the gift of anesthesia. Standing near the bed is my friend Charles, who made the trek to Houston and also made it his mission to ensure I receive the best care possible. He leans in as if he has a secret to tell me.

"You have Hodgkin's lymphoma, Katie. I've called your family. They are on their way."

Under the weight of the painkillers and sedatives, I can't seem to muster any emotion. I manage to smile through the cloud of uncertainty and follow the nurses' orders. They try to convince me to move and to drink some water. Moving isn't high on my priority list, though. I know the sooner I leave that bed, the sooner I face my reality.

⚾ ⚾ ⚾

Cancer survivors often talk about the moment their doctors uttered those painful three words: *"You have cancer."* Mine occurred unceremoniously, no doctors in sight. Instead, my big cancer reveal transpired under the bright lights of the surgical recovery room, while nurses force-fed me ice chips. Given the circumstances in which I'd been told, part of me wishfully thought, *Maybe it's all a bad dream.* Unfortunately, I learned later that night, after the drugs wore off, I now belonged to the group nobody wants to join—the cancer club.

I haven't written to you about it sooner because I couldn't bear to relive my worst nightmare. One thousand and twenty-one days and eleven hours after Dad had called me in the early morning hours to tell me you had died from cancer, I awoke from surgery and learned I had it too.

But once I knew what opponent I faced, I began to plan my offensive strategy. I decided to emulate the best pitchers—the ones who don't get rattled by external circumstances and who stand stoically on a fifteen-inch raised dirt mound on display, for all to see. They have a keen awareness of their strengths and understand how to manage their weaknesses. They don't let the strikes get them too pumped up, and they don't let the balls or, even worse, the wild pitches bring them down. They exude mental strength.

Over the next nine months, I treated every pitch I threw with great intention. I listened to the stats the experts rattled off. I paid attention to the pitches my trusted coaches suggested I throw. I read what others did in my situation. But in the end, I stood alone on that mound, with the game in my hands. And even though I had incredible teammates on the field to support me, this was my game to win or lose.

I wore a uniform, shirts that made it easy for the nurse to access my chemotherapy port. I listened to a playlist compiled by my "fans" to boost my spirits before game time. I painted my nails a new crazy color for each round. I packed healthy snacks and an attitude of "I've got this!" I found a way to have fun doing the least enjoyable thing I could ever imagine.

Even when round two nearly killed me.

My oncologist's physician's assistant decided to switch up my antinausea meds because the first round caused debilitating headaches. At first, all seemed to be going well. With the last drip of the IV, I threw my hand in the air with a fist pump. "Yes! Take that, cancer!" Two rounds down, six to go.

It turns out, I'd prematurely celebrated before the twenty-seventh out had been recorded.

The car ride home felt a bit blurry. The recognizable buildings on Holcombe Avenue became fuzzy concrete blocks. By the time the elevator door opened and I walked into my friend's apartment where I'd been living, I could barely stand. The room spun. I dropped my snack bag and clutched my stomach. I didn't say anything to anybody and attempted to walk to my bedroom, grabbing on to the hallway wall at times to steady myself.

Two minutes later, the lentils and veggies I'd eaten earlier reversed course, flying violently out of my mouth and all over the bathroom. A wave of clarity arrived in time for me to realize I needed to quickly reorient my body and direct my other end toward the toilet. And as violently as the food came out of my mouth, last night's grilled fish dinner came spewing out the other end, looking more like gulf water than the fish that swam in it.

The vomit/diarrhea biathlon lasted for hours with no end. Thank goodness for Rachel, who had followed me into the bathroom. There came a point when I couldn't lift my body off the floor, and I felt as if I might lose consciousness. I remember asking, "God, are you with me?" Immediately, I felt a presence and an overwhelming sense of peace. A feeling I had never known and had only read about in books.

I looked at Rachel and mumbled, "We need to get back to the hospital."

An IV of electrolytes and antinausea meds, a normal

bowel movement, and a 3:00 a.m. return home led to a much-needed night's sleep. The score: Chemo 2, Katie 0.

Other rounds weren't as eventful. Thanks to the right cocktail of steroids and antinausea meds and the shot of Neulasta I took to enhance my white blood cell count, the final scoreboard showed Katie 6, Chemo 2.

I kept up my pregame routine before each round and, before I knew it, five months passed and I rang the completion chemo bell.

While everyone in my life wanted to celebrate the final chemo treatment, a false sense of accomplishment lingered within me, as I knew another opponent awaited. I'd been careful to find small ways to celebrate along the way, but my focus never wavered. Like an ace pitcher, I told my team, "I'll go enjoy this one for the night, but then it's back to work tomorrow."

On my thirty-sixth birthday, I began radiation. Instead of a colorful cone-shaped birthday hat, I wore a mask so tight across my face it left lattice marks for hours after its removal. I lay half-naked, strapped to a cold table. The birthday suit irony wasn't lost on me. The bleomycin from the chemo had caused toxicity within my lungs, and I suffered from a dry cough that left me short of breath but not short on anxiety. It reached a zenith when the technicians became frustrated with me because I couldn't hold my breath long enough to complete the CT scan. What should have taken thirty minutes took several hours.

⚾ ⚾ ⚾

I never liked roller coasters. I'd sit on the park bench, eating cotton candy, waiting for all my friends to depart the ride and rejoin me. Then I'd relive their experience through their excitement. I preferred to have two feet on the ground, delighting in life's carnival culinary pleasures rather than being subjected to fabricated fear through steep slopes and inversions.

The ultimate roller coaster? Cancer. One minute, you receive good news. The next, your doctor says, "Katie, we see a spot on your scan." When you think you're nearing the end, you realize the most harrowing part is yet to come. I tried to find gratitude at every twist and turn, every test, every needle stick. But radiation challenged me and felt like an uphill climb.

With each appointment, my throat closed in, making meals extremely painful to eat. The side effects of being radiated from seven different angles for seventeen days straight wore on me physically and emotionally. While holding my breath as the lasers beamed through my body, I'd remind myself of who I wanted to be in the tough times. *You're a ballplayer, Katie. And when the game is on the line, you're the person who wants the ball. You've got this.*

I did have it. Being strong has little to do with your muscular strength. Lord knows my muscles had atrophied significantly. In fact, even though I weighed one hundred and five pounds, my DEXA scan classified me as obese due to my muscle-to-fat ratio. But I had abundant inner strength. You taught me how to be that way, Mom. Whenever life got hard, you'd say, "Toughen up, kid. You've got this." Much of my strength throughout that life-altering ordeal came from you, without you ever setting foot in MD Anderson.

Eight long months after beginning treatment, I had my last night of radiation. I said farewell to the nurses who'd cared so well for me, especially Loven and Lizabeth. I kept thinking back to Lou Gehrig's 1939 farewell to baseball speech. You know the one.

"I consider myself the luckiest man on the face of the earth." I pictured the Iron Horse as he stood near home plate. I knew I had a lot to live for. In the end, the worst thing that ever happened to me turned out to be the luckiest.

I don't ever want to forget my cancer experience, and I probably won't. I've always had a good memory. I know, I know—that bothered you. You once told me (likely after I reminded you of a past misstep you'd made), "You know, Katie, you could stand to forget a few things." I agree. I think we'd all benefit from not holding on too tightly to the past experiences that weigh us down and prevent us from moving forward. However, I also believe in exceptions.

I hope I always remember what I endured during my

cancer journey. I cherish the lessons I learned and the perspective I developed. Out of the unknown came patience. Out of the fear came faith and an acknowledgment that I'm connected to something bigger than myself. And out of the struggle came an understanding that while I am not in control of what happens to me, I *am* in control of my response.

Now, when faced with challenging life events, I'm the pitcher on the mound. I channel that unpredictable and scary time in my life and the gift of internal resolve it gave me.

I am okay. I am brave. I am strong.

XO,

KATIE

20

BE Calm

DEAR MOM,

You sat in a navy-blue, steel-legged school chair on the out-skirts of my read-aloud carpet. Twenty-one fourth graders settled in between us, eagerly awaiting my picture book reveal. This was your first visit to my classroom.

We gathered that day on the carpet to learn the lessons of *Thunder Cake*, an autobiography by Patricia Polacco, one of my favorite children's book writers. Polacco wrote many books about her childhood and the family members who influenced her. *Thunder Cake* tells the story of her and her grandma, Babushka's, responses to an ominous storm. Ten-year-old Polacco's reaction? Hide under the bed. Grandma's reaction? Bake a cake.

In the middle of the brewing storm, while others readied by shuttering their homes, Babushka prepared the ingredients to bake a Thunder Cake. Immersed in the rich language and beautiful imagery of Polacco's picture book, we learned about fears and the choices we have in overcoming them. As I facilitated our class discussion, I noticed you glowing, pride beaming from your permanent smile. The first opportunity you had without my students close by, you blurted, "You are the most incredible teacher!" Embarrassed by your comment being loud enough for everyone in the lunch break room to hear, I deflected the attention. "I am merely a reflection of my amazing students and their big hearts." Secretly, though, making you proud meant everything to me at age twenty-two (it still does).

Although you didn't say it during our class discussion, I knew you would've handled the impending storm exactly like Babushka. In fact, I don't even have to speculate. I have proof.

During the summer of 1995, we lived in Dad's childhood home—a pale-yellow shotgun house with rooms arranged one behind the other and doors at each end of the house. Its peeling exterior paint revealed haphazard brown streaks of exposed wood. I thought it needed a paint job, but you assured me, "It has a nice patina."

Our home still had its original, paper-thin glass windows, and they rattled every time the streetcar clambered down St. Charles Avenue two blocks away. I was home from college and eager to leave town as the last days of summer dragged on. The end of summer in New Orleans also meant the height of hurricane season.

One morning, Rachel and I awoke to almond croissants and breaking news banners on the television warning residents of New Orleans to be on alert for Hurricane Erin. "You two stop worrying. We'll be fine," you said. Rachel and I looked at you with skepticism, abandoned our half-eaten pastries on the kitchen island, and began preparing.

First, Rachel collected all of her stuffed animals and placed them in a garbage bag. Next, she moved her pile of clothes on the floor to the top shelf of her closet. This marked the only time I'd ever seen her voluntarily picking up her stuff. Finally, we taped our nine-pane windows with big Xs, protecting each rectangle from the strong winds. It looked like our house had been overrun with giant tic-tac-toe boards.

We marched on with a sense of urgency and headed straight for your room. We stood at your bedroom door, armed with two rolls of masking tape, ready to tackle another set of windows. Inside the room, instead of preparing for the storm, you sat on your couch reading the *Times-Picayune*. All three of the bedroom windows gaped open, and your thin brown hair danced across your face. "Come in—doesn't the breeze feel wonderful?"

Beyond those open windows, the entire neighborhood was on alert. Neighbors drove their cars onto the neutral ground, hoping the raised, grassy medians would protect them from flooding. You, however, chose to enjoy the fresh air, relaxing and reading the sports section. "Girls, we've been through many hurricanes before, and we'll make it through this one too."

As Hurricane Erin spun in the gulf, you stood on one side of the proverbial neutral ground. Rachel and I occupied the other. Dad, per the usual, straddled both positions, agreeing the breeze felt nice while simultaneously checking the batteries in all of his flashlights.

Luckily for us and flood-prone New Orleans, the hurricane turned east and barely impacted us. That is, aside from having to untape all of the windows and return Rachel's stuffed animals to their natural habitat. I was grateful that you never said, "Told you so."

During my stop at Citi Field to see the New York Mets play, I decided to climb all the way up to the highest point in the ballpark with my friend Bridget. As we ascended the concrete stairs, I remember thinking, *How can you even see the game from up here?* As we reached the nosebleeds, I realized we could see everything—every player, every inch of the field, every seat. The bird's-eye view revealed a cool mowed-in logo in the middle of the outfield strategically surrounded by a checkered pattern that must have taken the grounds crew hours to perfect. In contrast to the noise of

the game down below, up there, serenity. Experiencing the ballpark in that way made me realize the gift of perspective.

Little did I know when I snapped a bird's-eye photograph of the field, I captured Mets pitcher Noah Syndergaard on what would become a record-breaking night. Underneath the bright lights, he struck out a career-high thirteen players. Hours before he took the mound, Syndergaard learned that fellow starting pitcher Steven Matz had been placed on the disabled list. In the midst of an unexpected storm for his team, he struck out every member of Arizona's starting lineup at least once. After the game, a reporter asked him about his stellar performance. "I was able to just relax and go right after guys," he said.

Maybe there *is* something to that relaxing thing you, Babushka, and Syndergaard do in the midst of a squall? All three of you brought perspective to a trying time. Zoom out from the chaos. Consider the bigger picture. Breathe. And act. Or maybe, you know, don't act!

If I could go back to my classroom on the day you told me I was an incredible teacher, I would change what I said to you. "I am merely a reflection of you, Mom. *You* are the most incredible teacher. Among many other lessons, you taught me the power of perspective."

I regret that I didn't tell you sooner.

XO,
KATIE

21

BE Alert

JULY 11

CLEVELAND INDIANS – PROGRESSIVE FIELD

Mom,

I should have known something was wrong with me long before I landed in the hospital.

A weird pressure in my chest tried to tell me every time I did Pilates. I chalked it up to acid reflux, even though I hadn't suffered from it previously. Many mornings, my stomach shouted at me as I curled into a ball either in bed or on the bathroom floor. I figured my late-night pizza indulgence after my evening class let out at 10:00 p.m. caused the pain. Perhaps the biggest sign? While sleeping, I'd often sweat through my pajamas, waking up in a puddle. But anyone would if they had to get done what I had to for work and school in the next twenty-four hours. Anxiety and panic attacks hijacked my daily life.

I ignored it all.

At the Cleveland game, the boys sitting in the front row

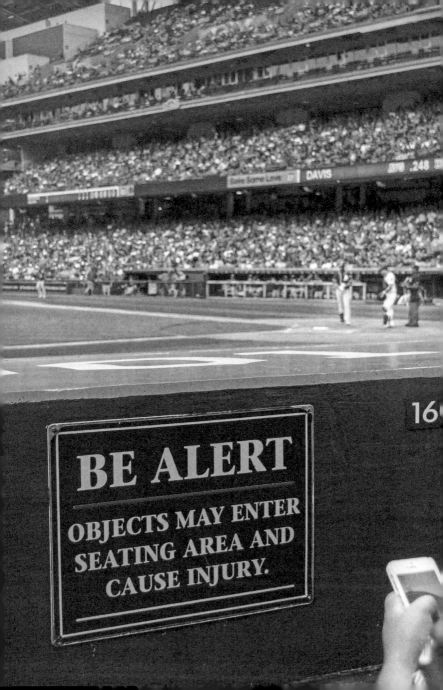

BE ALERT

OBJECTS MAY ENTER
SEATING AREA AND
CAUSE INJURY.

ignored it all too. They rarely looked up from their smart-phones, only glancing at the field on an occasion to heckle a player walking back to the dugout. In the second inning, I wanted to lean down and say, "Pay attention to the sign, boys! There's a left-handed batter at the plate. If he's late getting his bat around, the ball is heading your way at over one hundred miles per hour."

I didn't, for fear of sounding like an old fuddy-duddy. And it wouldn't have mattered, at least not that inning. Davis struck out looking. While the boys got lucky that time, I wanted them to know life sometimes doesn't work out that way.

I think you'd agree.

⚾ ⚾ ⚾

Who goes to Cabo in mid-August? We do! The unbearable heat made for some great travel deals. We met Rachel in the Houston Hobby airport, and all three of us boarded a flight to Mexico. The last trip we'd take together before your cancer diagnosis.

I arranged for a car to drive us to the hotel. As we exited the airport, a man holding a Russell sign greeted us in front of a limousine. I swore to you I had no idea it would be a limo. If you're still wondering, I *promise* I didn't know. You secretly loved it, and we giggled as we ducked into the silver stretch sedan. You unknowingly had matched your head-to-toe, peachy-orange plane outfit to the fluorescent lights lining the limo's ceiling.

We sipped welcome margaritas and, later that night, ate dinner on the beach under the starry sky at The Office. On the way there, we stopped for a predinner cocktail. Sweaty and tired from our uphill walk, we trailed behind as you marched right into world-famous Cabo Wabo. Without hesitation, you pointed at the gigantic special drink and said, "I'll have one of those!" The waiter paused. "Are you sure, ma'am?" Sensing a challenge, you said, "Of course," and downed that tequila-based fruity concoction like a boss, bifocals perched on your nose. You showed that twentysomething-year-old!

Most of the trip, you could find us poolside playing games: Scrabble, cards, and Pass the Pigs, to name a few. We kept track of our matches with a blue Vis-à-Vis pen and a laminated scoreboard I made prior to the trip. In between turns, we ate our way through the menu. Remnants of guacamole and chip grease on the rolling pigs *might* have altered their landing position a time or two.

Do you want to know my favorite part of the trip? Putt-Putt!

One afternoon, we tired of magazine flipping, dice rolling, and wave watching and decided to try our luck at mini golf. You jumped up from your poolside chaise and announced, "To the greens we go!"

Arguably, the putting greens provided the best view in the whole place. Located on the waterfront and raised a bit off the beach, I considered it prime real estate. It's the closest we've come to feeling like we've golfed at Pebble Beach. Spectacular view aside, the course paled in comparison to FunTime USA of Gulfport, Mississippi. No crazy caricatures, purple dinosaurs, or windmills. Flat greens as far as the eye could see.

Going into the final hole, the score stood tied. The Cabo Putt-Putt Open 2005 came down to your final stroke. Sink the putt, you'd win. You positioned your flip-flops about hip-width apart (you know, the ones with the banana-yellow squishy sole and pastel-rainbow canvas material between the toes). You eyed the hole through your glasses, drew your club straight back, and struck the ball. The line looked true but, lucky for me, the ball leaked to the right just before the hole. A congratulatory handshake followed, but I knew you extended it begrudgingly. Competitiveness runs in the family.

We doused our competitive fires by dipping our toes in the water as we strolled along the beach. The hotel warned against swimming in the water, but we didn't realize the red flag also meant even ankle-deep water would wreak havoc. That is, until a large wave roared ashore and the undertow swept your flip-flop right off your foot. You attempted to bend down and grab it, but at the exact same time, a new

wave swept in and sucked your flip-flop out to sea. Its buoy-
ant sole made for a makeshift boat, and we could see the
wayward thong bobbing atop the waves, heading farther
and farther into the Sea of Cortez.

First Putt-Putt. Then your flip-flop. Your losses
wouldn't end there.

On our way back to the room, I noticed the universal
hurricane symbol on the fitness room television. I casually
mentioned it to you. You laughed and brushed it off as me
being a worrywart. "Katie, don't be ridiculous. There's no
hurricane headed for us. We would know. The hotel would
tell us. I'll bet you ten dollars you're wrong."

Later that evening, the hotel slid a piece of paper under
the door: *Warning: Hurricane Hilary.* I resisted saying,
"Told you so!" Even though the hurricane tracked off shore
and paralleled the Baja coast, the outer bands proved strong
enough to do serious damage. Around midnight, the persistent and uncontrollable rattle of the balcony doors alerted
us to Hilary's arrival. We didn't sleep. At breakfast, through
weary eyes, we found the restaurant windows completely
blown out and glass scattered across the property. Small
trees had been uprooted and plants had lost their homes.

You paid up.

A couple of weeks later, our home took a direct hit from
one of the most destructive natural disasters in United
States history. Hurricane Katrina pounded the Louisiana

and Mississippi coast, and you lost more than a flip-flop. You lost everything.

I'll never forget what you said over the phone when you learned there was nothing left.

"Darn it, Katie! I missed the signs. I should have known losing my flip-flop and the hurricane in Mexico were trying to tell me something. I needed to learn how to detach from my things."

If you had known the flip-flop loss and brush with a hurricane foreshadowed what was to come, would it have changed your choices? There's no controlling nature. Katrina's path was set long before the meteorologists charted its course. Maybe you would have grabbed more things from the house—the things that really mattered to you? I know you felt enormous guilt for not doing so.

At the game in Cleveland, the baseball boys chose to ignore the signs and were spared the danger of a foul ball, for that game at least. Fate didn't leave you as fortunate.

In my case, had I sought medical help sooner, my entire life would have been altered.

If I had paid closer attention to the signs, it could have saved me from enduring a grueling cancer treatment that has since left my lungs scarred and my arterial walls prematurely aged. But then maybe I wouldn't have gone on this journey?

I don't know.

What I do know is that I don't want to live with the ultimate thief of time and joy—regret. I choose now to move through life consciously. Sometimes I'll notice the signs, and sometimes I probably won't. But I know if I remain alert, I'll be rewarded with a more thoughtful and examined life.

Sounds a lot like something you would say, Mom.

XO,
KATIE

22

BE Reflective

JULY 27

TEXAS RANGERS – GLOBE LIFE PARK

Hey, Mom. Can we talk about Dad?

I walked into Globe Life Park for the Rangers game when I noticed a statue. It depicted a father and child looking lovingly at each other as they walked hand in hand out of the ballpark. I noticed it only after I had entered and looked back. Isn't it interesting how looking back can often reveal something you easily missed? It triggered a flood of thoughts about Dad.

I don't have to tell *you* that hundreds of people in New Orleans loved Dad. We both often witnessed his fans' adoration. Ask the cab driver who picked me up one early morning to drive me to the airport. Dad walked me to the cab and put me inside to demonstrate to the driver that someone knew my whereabouts. He had barely opened the yellow door when the driver exited the taxi. "Dr. Russell? Is that you? I've been looking for you!"

141

He hugged Dad and, before I knew it, Dad had given the driver his personal cell phone number so he could call anytime he needed. During the entire drive out to the Louis Armstrong New Orleans International Airport, I listened to what felt like an introduction to Dad's lifetime achievement award speech. The driver summarized his thoughts with the last thing he said to me before I left the cab. "Your dad is the greatest."

I agreed.

As a child, I thought he personified perfection. While you often raised my anxiety, he calmed it. No matter the circumstances, I knew Dad would be Steady Eddie. And I could count on him to fix whatever was broken—my Walkman, a pounding headache, or even my science project. For my arctic diorama, he carved a polar bear out of a bar of Dial soap. My teacher commented on its impressiveness. I didn't give away his trick—he used coffee grounds for the eyes.

One summer, I curled up in my bed with a stomachache. I made myself sick with anxiety about boarding a plane by myself to fly to camp in North Carolina. Dad rubbed my back and whispered, "I'll drive you." To him, the twenty-hour, round-trip drive was worth it if it put me at ease.

Dad's small stature contrasted with his humongous heart. For most of my childhood, I heard stories from your friends about how he made house calls in the middle of the night, even on Christmas. If someone was in need, Dad showed up. For everyone.

This is why it surprised me when he failed to show up for *me* during cancer treatment.

If I grabbed your attention through sports, I grabbed Dad's attention by being sick. Caring for people made him tick. As a result, I may have exaggerated an illness a few times. Dad never questioned me, though. He would take me to his office and prop me up on his navy-blue, single-cushioned couch. He snuggled me in with three pillows and the white afghan a patient had given him for Christmas. Even the itchy wool didn't bother me. I *loved* being at the office with Dad.

I remember one day, I lay on the couch all morning with Rabbie, reading my Archie comic books. I felt safe knowing Dad was nearby. Attention from him didn't run short that day. I officially had become one of Dad's patients. At lunchtime, Mrs. Songy, his nurse, asked me what I wanted for lunch. Obviously, the best medicine for a sick child who couldn't make it to school was a hamburger with BBQ sauce and shredded cheddar cheese.

Dad joined us in the break room midway through my burger and fries. I considered myself lucky because Pat, his receptionist, whispered to me when he sat down to eat, "He *never* eats lunch." On a more typical day, he might grab a pastry from the McKenzie's Bakery box (which usually a patient or drug company rep had dropped off that morning), follow that with a cup of his favorite café au lait, and head right off to see the next patient.

Twenty-five years later, after the doctors officially diagnosed me with Hodgkin's lymphoma, Charlotte dragged Dad onto a plane (flying made him anxious) so they could join me in Houston. I loved having both of them with me in those first few days after my diagnosis and surgery. Like so many years ago in his office, I felt better knowing Dad was nearby.

After that trip, I didn't see Dad for eight months.

But looking back now, I think I understand why.

One year after I completed my treatment, as I mentioned in my earlier letter to you, Dad suffered a massive heart attack in Charleston, South Carolina, while on vacation. I sat outside of his hospital room while the nurse changed his catheter. I could hear Dad tell the nurse about each of his kids. When he spoke of me, he said, "Katie, she had cancer. We didn't know if she would make it."

My first clue revealed.

The fear of me possibly dying had paralyzed him. Dad spent two years caring for you, watching your body and mind deteriorate. He identified as a doctor, first and foremost. He saved people's lives. He was good at it, and that's how he has measured his worth. But he couldn't save you, Mom. The one thing he could always do, he couldn't. I don't think he could bear to watch his daughter die after losing you. Not on his watch.

My second clue came when I traveled to a wellness spa to spend time in the desert with Melissa and continue my post-cancer healing journey. I needed a thorough cleanse from all the trauma I'd experienced over the previous year. I signed up with a healer whose book I'd read prior to the trip. She survived cancer herself, and at the start of our session, I shared my story with her. After balancing my chakras with crystals, she leaned in and said, "You know your dad couldn't be present, and it's not because he doesn't love you, right?"

I hadn't even mentioned Dad to her. Yet she confirmed my hunches about Dad's absence from my cancer journey.

As I reflect on his actions, or lack thereof, during my cancer treatment, I have enormous empathy for what it must have been like for him. I've never questioned Dad's love for me. I only wish he could have loved *himself* more. If he better understood that his worth derives from more than how many lives he saves or how many acts he performs, maybe he would have spent more time nurturing himself instead of all his patients.

I wonder, how would that have changed his relationship with us?

XO,

KATIE

23

BE Grateful

AUGUST 4

LOS ANGELES ANGELS – ANGEL STADIUM

Ugh, Mom,

There are few things I dislike more than throwing up. I think it's why I never overindulged in drinking alcohol during college. The battle to hold everything in, despite my body's overwhelming desire to do otherwise, drained me. As a child, during such times, you held back my platinum-blonde hair while also securing a cold washcloth to my forehead. The towel served double duty as a fever reducer and a quick face cleaner. Afterward, I'd collapse in your arms until I had enough energy to return to your bed and my stuffed animals. Rabbie guarded the copper kitchen pot you'd placed on top of the comforter, in case I couldn't make it to the bathroom.

I could've used some of your magic touch, Mom, one early Monday morning during my PhD program. I lay on the bathroom floor with pain in my stomach so fierce it pinned me down. I'd thrown up a couple of times already, which seemed to be a repeat of the previous week, when I'd eaten what must have been an undercooked rotisserie chicken. It's hard to be sick alone.

The week prior, after my last episode of vomiting, I ate a BRAT diet (bananas, rice, applesauce, toast). I'd felt fine for several days, so I decided to get out of the house for the first time all week. I called my friend Elizabeth and asked if she wanted to go to church with me. While baptized and confirmed in the Episcopal Church, I hadn't been since I moved to Austin several years prior (other than for Christmas and Easter holidays).

We chose the early evening service, and it reminded me of the peace and connection I feel when worshiping in community with others. Overwhelmed with gratitude for that time and for my health, I practically bounced out of the chapel and into the parking lot after the service. I dropped Elizabeth off at her home in South Austin and picked up an aptly named Crossroads taco from a food trailer park nearby. I had no idea that decision would have far-reaching consequences.

Turns out, a brisket taco with jalapeños wasn't the best choice after experiencing food poisoning symptoms one week prior. But I felt fine when I placed the order. The next morning, my stomach reported otherwise. I had a second date with the tile floor and the porcelain goddess—out once again.

⚾ ⚾ ⚾

Mom, do you know what happens more in a baseball game than anything else (except pitches)?

Outs!

Every game guarantees at least fifty-one of them (barring a rainout). In no other sport are your failures on such prominent display. At Angel Stadium, I saw a whole lot of outs and not much else.

Despite Cleveland Indians pitcher Carlos Carrasco allowing only one hit, the game went into extra innings, tied 0–0. A twelfth-inning, walk-off home run ended the pitching duel, but the highlight for me happened to be a strikeout. In the bottom of the fourth, I put myself in the perfect position to catch Albert Pujols's appearance at the plate. I hoped to capture his next dinger on video.

He struck out, adding one more strikeout to his career total of over a thousand.

In the 1999 draft, MLB teams selected 401 players before Pujols. Yet he's become a top ten all-time home run hitter. What are the chances he would land on a list with the all-time greats, the likes of Barry Bonds, Hank Aaron, and Babe Ruth? The scouts didn't believe it possible. But I bet Pujols did.

That's what disappointment and strikeouts can do for you. They place you on a different path, if you allow them.

It's the strikeouts that coach you to make a change. The best players learn from the outs and use them as a guide to hitting home runs.

Food poisoning, like outs in a baseball game, may have some advantages.

A phone call to Dad, who suggested I needed to seek medical attention, and a short car ride from my next-door neighbor to the emergency room, landed me in the hospital for a three-day stay. Who gets hospitalized three days for food poisoning? My bloodwork markers for inflammation measured extremely high, and my CT scan revealed a severe infection in my small intestines. The doctors gave me antibiotics and antinausea drugs but didn't fully understand what the numbers indicated. Many of them thought I had Crohn's disease, despite my assurances that I had never experienced bowel issues and had no family history.

I tried to tell the attending physician that I felt something in my chest. He dismissed it and said, "You're too young for heart trouble." I felt like saying, "What about babies born with congenital heart defects who require surgery within the first hours of their lives? Are they too young?!"

I wish he would have listened.

If he'd acted on my symptoms, maybe he would have ordered the CT scan not only of my abdomen but also of my chest. If he'd asked the radiology technician to move the doughnutlike ring six inches higher, the doctors would have discovered the mass encapsulating my coronary artery.

Despite not knowing what was actually going on in my body, I knew something was wrong. The universe had hit me upside the head two weeks in a row and sent a loud and clear message: *You are not okay.* Upon my release from the hospital, I couldn't get access to the recommended gastroenterologist in Austin for over a month. A strikeout that would later prove to be lifesaving.

With help from a friend, I arranged to see the best gastroenterologist in Houston the following week. I packed my bags for a night and headed east. Turns out, I should have packed Bonnie's steamer—I could have used a more extensive wardrobe. I ended up staying in Houston for nine months. You know the rest of the story.

At first, I thought an undercooked rotisserie chicken and slices of jalapeño brisket had joined forces against me. In reality, that bird and that cow saved my life.

The opportunity for gratitude exists in every moment, and blessings truly can be disguised.

Even ones that appear in the form of a taco.

XO,

KATIE

24

BE Forgiving

AUGUST 9

SAN DIEGO PADRES – PETCO PARK

Mom,

Southern California's laid-back reputation was on full display at Petco Park. Fans in flip-flops and board shorts drank from a wide variety of local craft beers, while others stood in line for a coveted burgundy BBQ tri-tip sandwich from Cardiff's famed Seaside Market. Beyond the outfield wall, kids built sandcastles on a man-made beach and imitated their favorite players in a pickup game of Wiffle ball on a miniature field. It's always sunny at Petco despite the play on the field or the Padres' record, which never seemed to be very good. When I visited, they'd only recorded fourteen winning seasons since their inception in 1969, and that day turned out to be more of the same. The Phillies, who were in last place in *their* division, handed the Padres their sixth straight loss and swept the series.

Baseball isn't the only place where bad games or even unfortunate seasons happen. Life isn't perfect and neither were you—nor am I. Still, I hesitated to write you this letter. Addressing your missteps is uncomfortable. You never wanted to talk about them in the first place. I do, though.

Deep breath. Here goes.

Mom, if the holidays inspired your most creative and spirited self, they also left you at your most vulnerable to crash. During my sophomore year in college, I flew home to spend the winter holidays with the fam. Christmas evoked

154

an entire range of emotions for you, but this one seemed to be more challenging than most. Earlier in the year, you and Dad had decided to live in separate homes as you struggled to make sense of your relationship. You placed high expectations on yourself for the week, knowing the entire family would be together, including Dad. You cooked for days (all of our favorites) and planned activities to ensure a perfect holiday season. From cookie baking to pizza making, ornament shopping to Galatoire's lunching, you wanted the week to be festive and fun.

Your carefully laid plans didn't unfold exactly as scripted, however. Instead of eating your butterscotch brownies, we wanted beignets. Instead of leftovers, we wanted Camellia Grill waffles and chocolate freezes. We wanted to spend time with our friends. All of the anticipation and energy you put toward making Christmas "just right" inevitably left you disappointed and depleted.

The night after Christmas began mundanely but didn't remain that way for long. Rachel and I both stayed home to play spades with you. For dinner, Rachel wanted pasta. Shocker! She exclusively ate spaghetti in high school and had graduated from buttered noodles to pasta and Prego. You started preparing her meal and asked me if I wanted some. I did not. While I supported Rachel's leap forward to eating processed tomato sauce, I preferred your fresh tomatoes and basil.

"I *guess* I'll have to make you something different since you're too good to eat Prego." You begrudgingly sliced super-ripe Creole tomatoes for me. Funny thing is, I didn't ask you to make me anything. And wasn't it *you* who taught me that fresh produce reigns supreme to canned, bottled, or frozen?

I remember wanting to say to Rachel, "Ruh-roh—she's about to lose it. This is the captain speaking: we have lost cabin pressure."

Spades never happened that night. The preparation of two separate dinners—and the emotional release of Christmas ending—led to an epic meltdown. You screamed at me, "You are so difficult!" And the next thing out of your mouth was a real doozy. Wait for it . . .

"You ruined my entire life."

Yep! You read that right, and you didn't stop there. The verbal beatdown continued. Meanwhile, I told myself your behavior had nothing to do with me. You were irrational, and I had witnessed the not-so-merry-Christmas meltdown Mom before. I knew. Best to listen and keep my mouth shut.

You managed to put plates in front of us, one with Prego and one with fresh tomatoes. I ate nothing. I may have been strong, but I wasn't bulletproof. I wiped away my tears with my sweatshirt cuff and hung my head. You didn't notice because you stormed out of the kitchen, and we didn't see you again that night—or for the next few days. This was how these things went.

The physical and emotional energy you invested in preparing for Christmas and trying to make things perfect for everyone else left you without much for yourself. The result? You crashed and then locked yourself in your room with your novels and newspapers. You never acknowledged it, but depression grasped you in its tight grip, and it took days to loosen it.

While these episodes occurred infrequently, even the rare crashes left me wondering what role I played in your unhappiness. Of course, I felt responsible. How could I not? You had told me I was to blame. I've realized in the years since, this most definitely wasn't about me. And it wasn't about Christmas either. It was about how becoming a mom completely changes a woman's life. I imagine there were some dreams you deferred. Certainly, there were daily sacrifices. It couldn't have been easy.

When the fog cleared, you emerged from your bedroom and life went back to "normal." Yet the haze of unspoken apologies remained. Forgiveness can't be granted without conversation. I knew your conscience overflowed with guilt and shame. Instead of dialogue, you'd double down on trying to please us through food, your preferred love language. "Want me to go get you a Bud's Broiler—number four, special sauce, no onions?" (You knew that was my favorite.)

I wanted to say, "No, my stomach is full. What needs feeding is my broken heart."

But you pretended like nothing happened. I wish we could have talked about those moments more. Imagine what kind of healing we could have experienced.

Your highs were high and your lows low. I'd fallen victim to your mood swings enough to know I never wanted to emulate that part of you. I've worked hard learning how to acknowledge and talk about my emotions, given that I never had any model for what that looked like. The lack of communication within our family prevented me from being the best version of myself for a long time. Now, I understand that when we don't take care of ourselves, we take out our unresolved emotions on others. I wasn't responsible for your happiness, but I *am* responsible for mine.

Mom, I forgive you. For all of your bad games. For all of the seasons when you weren't at your best. On occasion, you dropped the ball, but even the pros do that.

Will you promise me one thing?

When I see you again one day, can we never again let silence prevail?

XO,
KATIE

25

BE Balanced

AUGUST 26

DETROIT TIGERS – COMERICA PARK

Mom,

You would have been on the edge of your seat, ready to record this game in the history books. No way you would have left early! Justin Verlander stood on the mound, three outs away from potentially adding his name to the select group of five pitchers who'd completed three no-hitters. Meanwhile, the Angels' Chris Iannetta stood at the plate, hoping to get his team's first hit of the night.

With each pitch, the ballpark decibel level climbed. Fans sensed the history in the making, with the bottom of the order up and Iannetta only hitting .188. Verlander went after him with his fastball, which he'd been dealing all night. The first two missed outside of the zone. Iannetta fouled off the third pitch. Behind in the count, Verlander took a little something off the next one, throwing him a slider and getting him to chase on a low, outside pitch. Count 2–2.

A stunning performance, considering how far Verlander had come that season. He began it on the disabled list and didn't have his first start until June. He struggled to return to form, recording only two wins in twelve games. No matter your allegiance, if you love baseball, you couldn't help but root for a pitcher to mark his comeback with a no-hitter. And perhaps we rooted, selfishly, for our own opportunity to be part of something historic.

Though everyone seemed fixated on Verlander, I couldn't help thinking about Iannetta and what it meant for him to be in the batter's box to start off the ninth. Many sports reporters write about the mental toughness it takes for a pitcher to throw a no-hitter, but rarely do people talk about the hitter's mental state in that situation. My heart started pounding, imagining myself in Iannetta's cleats, knowing how conflicted my thoughts would be.

My competitive voice would come out hollering: *Come on, Katie, get a hit—line drive in the gap. Let's get this guy; he's running out of gas.* But quickly thereafter, my empathetic voice would reply, *Katie, you don't want to be the person who takes the no-hitter away from Verlander. Maybe he'll walk you so you get on base. That way you're not responsible for ruining his chances.*

I'm fairly certain Iannetta, or any other Major League Baseball player, doesn't subscribe to empathizing with another team's pitcher. But for as long as I can remember, I've lived with those voices inside my head, competing between thinking of myself and thinking of others. I likely got that from you and Dad. I'm not convinced either of you ever learned how to prioritize your own needs.

On a 2–2 count, Verlander went back to his fastball and left it hanging right over the heart of the plate. Iannetta hit a line drive to left field. Verlander and fans leaned in, fixated on the ball's trajectory. It plunked down on the line, inches from being foul. Verlander's bid for his third no-hitter went up in a cloud of chalk. A collective "ugh," led by Verlander, could be heard throughout Comerica, followed by clapping and a standing ovation. He retired the next three batters.

Verlander's perspective after the game? "It happens." He spoke like a veteran pitcher with experience going deep into games, with no-hitters on the line that didn't come to fruition. While he may not have achieved a no-hitter, he still logged a one-hit complete game. Perhaps even better than that, he finally regained his confidence and command of his fastball. His critics had been relentless and the doubters vocal. Now, a near no-hitter catapulted him into a different conversation, silencing the rumors that his best pitching was behind him. While his velocity had been down from previous years, that night he artfully balanced his fastball with his slider, curve, and changeup.

Baseball, after all, is a game of balance. Managers balance lineups with right- and left-handed hitters. Pitching coaches balance their bullpens with finesse pitchers and flamethrowers. Effective batters know you can't hit the ball with power if you're off balance. The season has over 160 games; the best teams realize you can't overinvest in any one game or one outcome.

You and I never mastered the balance thing while you were alive. As I already mentioned, we struggled with whom to prioritize—ourselves or others. I sometimes wonder if that's what caused our cancers. I'll never be able to draw causality, but I don't think it did us any favors. And Dad most definitely didn't model a healthy work-life balance. With you two as my parents, it should've come as no surprise that I became a teacher—a quintessential caring-about-others profession.

While I'm not a mom, I played a pseudomother to many of my fourth graders, especially those who lived in less-than-ideal home situations. Most days, I arrived at school by 6:30 a.m. and didn't leave till after 6:00 p.m. Fridays were the exception, when I left at 4:00 p.m. to attend happy hour at Chili's with my fellow teachers, Sarah, Bridget, and Amy. We spent what little money we had on bottomless chips and salsa and half-price margaritas. I'd be asleep by 7:00 p.m., catching up on a week's worth of missed Zs. On Saturday or Sunday, I'd return to campus, planning lessons, grading assignments, and thinking about my students.

Clearly, I lacked balance. I didn't have much self-awareness in my twenties, and I certainly didn't value the time I spent on my needs as highly as the time I spent taking care of others. By my midthirties, cancer came crashing into my life and forced me to take a long, hard look at my choices. I wanted to know why this had happened to me and how to keep it from returning.

I read voraciously. I learned about reducing inflammation, the power of meditation, and how to cultivate self-compassion. I went on health retreats and studied Ayurveda, an ancient healing science. I spent an entire year doing the Institute for Integrative Nutrition's online program and got certified as an integrative health coach. I began to say no to things I didn't want to do and yes to the things that sparked joy. I prioritized my sleep, and suddenly my energy increased. I asked for what I needed and became receptive to help. I set boundaries and spent less energy trying to fix others' problems. I let go of what some people thought of me and listened more to my own voice. I ate healthy foods and asked them to hold the dairy and gluten without worrying about the "high maintenance" label. I realized I *do* have fifteen minutes to spare in my busy day for stillness and started a meditation practice.

I won't tell you I did these things every day, but I had an awareness of what doing these things meant for my overall well-being. With cancer peering over my shoulder, I stayed disciplined and on the right path.

And, if you're wondering, of course I didn't stop thinking about or doing for others. At one point, I mentioned to my therapist my fear of tipping the scale too far in this new direction. He said, "No matter how much you take care of yourself, you're never going to stop thinking of others, Katie. You're wired to empathize." With a wry smile, he added, "But I'll be sure to let you know if I see you becoming self-absorbed."

For many years, I'd lived with the thought that compassion was a zero-sum game; compassion for myself could only come at the expense of compassion for others. That was far from the truth. I learned growing my self-compassion meant I had more compassion to go around.

I remain grateful to you and Dad for modeling what it looks like to throw love into the world. And I'm equally appreciative of the gift of cancer for reminding me that if you don't catch some things for yourself, you'll have nothing to throw back.

I know there will be games when I give up my at bat to move the runner to second. There will be times I dive for a ball, bruising my knee to get the out. I'm eager to be a team player in life. But if I'm not healthy enough to suit up, I'm never going to see the playing field.

That night in Detroit, sometime before the ninth inning, Iannetta turned his attention away from the game to watch a 2011 video with his hitting coach. That year, his batting average had been fifty points higher. He noticed a difference in his hand position and a more closed stance. A moment of self-awareness, something must have clicked. He took care of himself and, in turn, took care of his team.

XO,
KATIE

BE Still

AUGUST 28

TORONTO BLUE JAYS – ROGERS CENTRE

DEAR MOM,

Listening to the crowd noise might lead you to believe certain situations—full-count hits, tie-game home runs, bases-loaded strikeouts—determine a game's outcome. I, however, believe it's what happens between the pitches that matters most. After all, you don't get to those game-changing plays without the signs that preceded them.

Hundreds of baseball signs may be given and received during a game—catcher to pitcher, fielder to fielder, coach to hitter. This unspoken language communicates to a player what he's supposed to do with the ball or his bat and even his body. The execution of these strategies is critical to the team's success.

Yet most fans miss them.

Too busy chugging a beer, popping peanuts, or showing off their baseball knowledge to a seatmate, they overlook the game within the game. In fans' defense, signs are intentionally fast and sneaky because no player or manager wants the other team to discern them. Taps, tugs, and tips all choreographed in a matter of seconds. No body part is off limits in this dance—one of baseball's oldest and strangest rituals.

But the home run doesn't get hit, the strikeout never occurs, and the squeeze rarely works if managers and players don't effectively deliver and receive the signs. Kevin Pillar, Toronto's center fielder, added a stolen base to his stats when the third base coach gave him a "green light" sign to steal on the next pitch. Roberto Osuna struck out the side in the top of the ninth because the catcher communicated with his fingers the perfect location and type of pitch for each batter. As it turns out, signs occurred both on the diamond and in the stands that early evening as the Blue Jays played the Detroit Tigers.

The sold-out crowd for the fifth game in a row rocked the open-roofed Rogers Centre. The crowd sang along to the national anthems of both Canada and the United States. The guy next to me consumed one of his aggressively topped footlongs (he had another one on deck in his other hand), and both teams treated fans to a run in the first inning. Between innings, I closed my eyes and took a deep breath, attempting to soak up all the magic. I opened them in time to discover the jumbotron in center field posing the following question: *Who am I?*

Say what?

Three weeks prior I'd attended a weeklong experience at the Chopra Center, to learn more about cultivating a meditation practice to help manage my anxiety. I learned to incorporate this *exact* question at the start of my daily meditations. The words that had occupied my mind for twenty days straight suddenly occupied a giant screen in a baseball stadium! Now more than ever, I knew this pilgrimage was leading me down the long, winding path to the answer. This latest message quietly nudged me to keep asking the question.

I'd born witness to many signs throughout my journey, but in Toronto they seemed to be downloading fast and furious. The night before the game, I made a reservation for one at Luckee, located in the center of Toronto's entertainment district. Eating alone had become one of the many new habits I'd picked up along my ballpark route. I appreciated the heightened sensory experience that solitary dining offered. I noticed the details of the red light fixture, the floral scent of my cocktail, and the cold, smooth feel of the flatware in my hand. Details so easily missed without stillness.

While known for their dim sum and modern take on Chinese cuisine, it was Luckee's fortune cookie that stole the show. Housed in a bamboo steamer, I lifted the lid and unveiled yet another sign.

Traveling this year will put your life in great perspective.

I walked back to my hotel that night wondering, *How did a fortune cookie know my life seemed to be unfolding in ways I thought only happened in the movies?*

I awoke early the next morning, eager to get to the ferry dock, and I learned I wasn't the only person with that idea. I boarded the packed Centre Island Ferry, headed to the Toronto Islands with the rest of the adventure-seeking families. Thirteen minutes later, we'd been transported to an entirely different scene.

Tree-lined paths led to bridges over ponds. Kids scurried in the direction of the amusement park. A log ride, giant spinning bears, and bumper boats awaited their sticky hands. After snapping photos of idyllic park scenes, I located an empty bench, framed by trees and perched along the banks of Lake Ontario.

I lost track of time and sat on the bench for over an hour, listening to the faint sound of happiness behind me. Ahead, only a mile and a half away, skyscrapers stood and the CN Tower loomed. Nestled in the heart of the hustle and bustle of Canada's largest city sat Rogers Centre, Toronto's baseball oasis. And just beyond the shore, boats crisscrossed the lake. Ferries and Tiki Taxis shuttled visitors to and fro, while sailboats small and large tacked into the wind. In the sky, planes began their final descent and approach for landing at the Billy Bishop Regional Airport.

A lone kayaker floated into my line of sight. Tranquility

in a sea and scene of anything but. Yet another reminder that stillness can be found in any moment, even the most active and noisy ones. It's in those instances, Mom, when I feel connected to you. It must be why I lingered on that bench for so long.

After the game ended later that night, I left the Rogers Centre invigorated by the crowd and a home-team win. Basking in baseball's afterglow, it would have been easy to get caught up in the flow of people departing the game and miss him. Hundreds already had. An older gentleman, toes peeking out of a tennis shoe, sat in the middle of the sidewalk with his cap extended in the hopes of receiving a donation. I checked my purse and realized I didn't have any cash on me, so I thought about what else I had to give. I walked up to him, stopped, and flashed him my biggest smile, as fans rushed past both of us, eager to arrive at their next destination. He raised his head slightly as he smiled right back and said, "Thank you."

His smile changed me. It inspired me to never be without cash for someone in need. And it reminded me that it's the unspoken words, the gestures, the signs we give and receive in stillness, between the pitches, that might determine who wins after all.

XO,
KATIE

27

BE Loyal

Mom, do you remember Aramis Ramírez?

Surely you do. The fan-favorite played third base for the Cubs during the time you watched copious amounts of baseball while recovering from countless cancer procedures. In 2015, while playing for the Brewers, he was part of a late-season trade that sent him to the Pittsburgh Pirates. Ramírez had begun his career in Pittsburgh in 1998, and the trade allowed him to finish exactly where he had started.

The night I visited Milwaukee, the Brewers played the Pirates, with Ramírez on the roster. He'd recently announced his retirement, effective at season's end. During the pregame, I sat on the edge of my seat perplexed, wondering why the opposing team's manager stood beside Ramírez and posed for photographs. It turned out, Ramírez's former team honored him with the actual third base from his final game as a Brewer and a plaque listing his eighteen-year career accomplishments, which were abundant.

I cried. I didn't understand why. Was it my heightened hormones that liked to wreak havoc during "that time of the month"? Was I getting sentimental about my journey coming to an end, with only three games left? Was it a combination of the two, or something else altogether?

As the pregame announcer introduced Ramírez, the entire stadium stood and clapped.

It didn't matter which team you supported that night—we *all* rooted for Ramírez. We rooted for kindness and for the lasting connection we have with people, even when they're no longer on our team. Whether in sports, politics, or the workplace, honoring all human beings (especially those who aren't on our team) isn't the norm. That night, though, a rival team honored a former player. Friendships and connections superseded the scoreboard. While pregame rarely renders the stands full, my heart certainly was.

One of the greatest gifts of doing this baseball journey was the response of people in my life who might have been considered "no longer on my team." While technology increases both the ease and speed with which people connect to those from their pasts, I hadn't really boarded the social media train. That is, until I stepped out into the world and into America's ballparks.

Once the press began covering my journey, emails poured in.

It's been a long time since we connected.

_____

Although long time no see, I thought I would reach out.

_____

Too many years have passed since last connecting with you.

The well-wishes came from far and wide—teammates from high school, old coaches, friends from college, and former coworkers.

After attending the Red Sox game, I spent time in Cape Cod for the Fourth of July holiday. On my way there, I had lunch in Plymouth, Massachusetts. Known to most as the town where the Pilgrims landed in 1620 aboard the _Mayflower_, I knew Plymouth as the hometown of my favorite summer camper, Karyn Murray.

As you know, Mom, I spent the summers of my sophomore and junior years in college coaching at Spirit Sports Camp in Bridgton, Maine. A small lake community about an hour north of Portland, Bridgton had a way of making a trip to Dunkin' Donuts one town over feel like a big adventure for this city girl. It did, however, make the perfect setting for an all-girls summer sports camp. There, I met a totally rad teenager.

I taught Karyn, thirteen at the time, the intricacies of the windmill pitch and everything else I knew about softball. She would give me piggyback rides up the hill in the mornings. At night, I would braid her hair while we all hung out in the dorms, swapping sports stories. She nicknamed me Little Bitty. Although I was six years older, the top of my head barely reached her shoulder. We were inseparable that summer.

After camp ended, Karyn sent me a care package. Inside, Alan Jackson's sixth album rested in a bed of bubble wrap. I chuckled when I opened it. The first track? "Little Bitty!" I called to thank her, and we reminisced about our cutthroat capture-the-flag games and our epic bombardment competitions (think dodgeball but more intense). An hour later, we said goodbye.

Twenty years later, during my visit to Plymouth, Karyn's presence was strong. At lunch, I mentioned her to my friend Kate, while we waited for our burgers. I even thought, *Wouldn't it be neat if our paths randomly crossed while I was walking around town?*

They didn't, but I would soon think of Karyn again. Only a few months after my lunch in Plymouth, I learned from the Spirit Sports Camp website that she'd asked her wedding guests, in lieu of gifts, to donate to a camp scholarship fund she created. Karyn Murray . . . married? Gosh, I felt old! It wasn't surprising that she'd do such a thoughtful and selfless thing during a time when most people focus on themselves. Unbeknownst to Karyn, I made a donation.

Five months later, our paths did cross. Karyn emailed me.

Good morning, Katie,

You may not remember me, but it's Karyn Murray, I was a camper at Spirit Sports Camp way back in the '90s when you were a coach there. I am a nurse at Mass General Hospital in Boston now. The craziest thing happened at work the other day, and I felt compelled to reach out to you. Some colleagues and I were having a discussion about cancer in young people and one of my fellow nurses brought your story to my attention. She said she had seen this story about a woman traveling around to all the MLB ballparks in memory of her mom. Of course, with the internet she googled it so I could read the story. As I got to reading I saw a picture of you and I put two and two together and realized it was my long-lost Spirit coach!

I wanted to say I was sorry for the loss

of your mom and that the story of your own survival is inspiring to people. Especially young women all the way up in Boston. Keep up the good fight! Wishing you a happy and healthy 2016!

Best wishes,
Karyn

As the Brewers had done by honoring Ramírez, Karyn and I found a way to honor each other. What a beautiful thing to reconnect with old teammates and remember why we connected in the first place.

Even those we think we have lost touch with are forever a part of our team.

XO,
KATIE

28

BE Open

CAN YOU BELIEVE IT, MOM? ONLY TWO MORE BALLPARKS!

Angie, my friend from the doctoral program, drove over from Columbia, Missouri, to join me for the Royals game (rescheduled from earlier in the summer). We walked around the stadium indulging in all that Kauffman had to offer. We Putt-Putted, rode the baseball-themed carousel, and gobbled up some delicious Kansas City barbecue. Experiencing her first Major League Baseball game, Angie didn't want to miss a thing!

"What are they doing over there? What's that called? What happened?" She peppered me with questions. There's something special about seeing the game through a rookie's eyes.

There's also something special about witnessing a family interacting at a ballpark. In the seats in front of us, a mom had purchased a bag of cotton candy for her son. The joy and anticipation on the boy's face while opening the bag of pink-and-blue sugary goodness captivated me. I could almost taste it myself. Instead of using the pinch technique (the preferred method of Mardi Gras parade-goers), the boy dove in wide mouth first. Brilliant, if you ask me! His mom smiled and snuck her own piece of the sugar cloud. He glared at her and clutched his bag as if he'd been robbed. I captured it all on camera. The previous twenty-seven ballparks taught me it's the small things in and around a baseball game that make the best photos.

After an inning or two, I leaned over and showed them the series of shots. We chatted for a bit about my journey, and I shared my contact information. A few days later, I received an email from her. She wanted a digital copy of the photos, and she wanted to tell me something else. She, too, had recently graduated with her PhD and lost her mom to cancer. Upon reading my bio, even her husband remarked, "She sounds like you!"

I'd heard about people who were in the same place unknowingly and then met years later. A photograph or a story uncovered the happenstance. While not as dramatic, her email and our interaction at the ballpark that day reminded me of a lesson you taught me: *Stay open to what's directly in front of you and whose path you may be crossing.*

⚾ ⚾ ⚾

Baseball has given me many gifts, and I wanted to give back to baseball. I wanted to express my gratitude for the sport that had embraced me every step of the way—not only during my thirty-ballpark journey but throughout my life. At the same time, I considered the other important communities that shaped my identity. Top of the list? Pass Christian, the place where I learned to drive a tractor, where I built my first sandcastle, and where we gathered annually with friends and family to celebrate countless spring and summer holidays.

A quick internet search using the terms "baseball and Pass Christian," led me to the PC Pirates high hchool baseball page. I discovered that the booster club planned to hold a cornhole and cow drop fundraiser for the team. In only four days. A sign? A coincidence? I think we both know the answer.

I'd learned to be more open in my life and listened more carefully to what the universe had to say. Coupled with another lesson I learned from you—*be more spontaneous!*—I didn't hesitate. By day's end, I'd booked a flight, dragged out the ol' wooden cornhole boards, dusted off the beanbags, and started practicing. My main reason for going was to help them raise money, but it's virtually impossible to turn down my competitive dial.

I coerced Charlotte to be my partner, and the morning of the tourney, she drove from New Orleans to pick me up for the event. Pass Christian encompasses a little over fifteen square miles, and somehow we still managed to get lost. But our circuitous route was meant to be.

We pulled up to a stop sign we never would have encountered had we taken the direct route. Our first opportunity to engage with the community stepped out from behind a poster board. That opportunity sported ponytails. A group of young softball players encouraged motorists to donate money for their team. I rolled down the window and handed the girl a folded bill. As we drove away, we caught her reaction in the rearview mirror. She opened it, shouted, "Mom! Mom!" and ran across the street waving Andrew Jackson's face in the air. A loud "woohoo" could be heard from a block away.

Fifteen minutes later, we finally found the fundraiser. Cornhole boards of all colors and logos were lined up, awaiting the first beanbag thumps of the day. I bet you could predict what logos splashed across the field. If you guessed LSU Tigers and New Orleans Saints, you'd be correct. Wafts of jambalaya and two friendly ladies at the red-checkered registration table welcomed us, "How y'all doing?"

We bought our tickets for the cow drop (selecting a bingo square number where we thought the cow would drop his first poop) and secured a spot in the cornhole tourney. Pass Christian, population 5,463 plus 2. We knew not a single person and wondered if anyone noticed us. No one had any clue who we were or why we were there. Yet we felt like we belonged.

I chose the white boards painted with red baseball seams, hoping they'd bring us good luck. Wishful thinking. Ten minutes later, our tournament trophy hopes ended unceremoniously in the first round. Our opponents must have had more than four days to practice. At least that's what we told ourselves after the rout.

No longer in contention, we began to mingle and chat with folks. Unknowingly, we crossed paths with Coach Whitfield. Although we only spoke briefly, he spoke passionately about the team and the community and hoped the fundraiser might bring in enough money to build a wooden fence for their field. The current set-up meant base hits often disappeared into the dense Mississippi woods, never to be seen again.

Charlotte and I left that afternoon, licking our wounds and swallowing our pride. No, we didn't win the cow drop either! I also left with an overwhelming sense that wouldn't be the last of my interactions with the Pass Christian Pirates and Coach Whitfield.

I couldn't help but conjure up images of Kevin Costner in *Field of Dreams*. The entire flight back to Austin, my mind played on repeat, *"If we build it, they will come."*

On my flight, I drafted an email to my friends and

fellow baseball supporters. I also created a GoFundMe page for the PC baseball team. Our goal: raise $10,000 to build a fence. And come they did. Many of my friends who had experienced the magic of the Pass gladly participated. In a short amount of time, we reached our goal, Mom. Coach Whitfield and the Pirates got their new fence.

I thought I knew no one at the fundraiser. Turns out, I knew Coach Whitfield's story after all. I later learned that he, too, lost his mother from cancer when he was young. Yet another reminder, we are more alike than we are different.

The key is to remain open to the people who are right in front of us.

XO,
KATIE

29

BE in the Moment

SEPTEMBER 7

CHICAGO WHITE SOX – U.S. CELLULAR FIELD

Mom,

I landed at Midway Airport and hailed a cab to U.S. Cellular Field. Scenes from our '80s trip to Chicago to see the Cubs play flashed through my mind as the downtown skyscrapers loomed. In some ways, the White Sox have lived in the Cubs' shadow for their entire history. Even though I traveled to the Windy City that day to see the Sox, my attention turned to Wrigley and the game we watched together.

We sat in the bleachers—right field to be exact. I wanted to be close to my favorite player, Andre Dawson, the first player on a last-place team to win the MVP award. He might have been merely a right fielder to some, but to me, "the Hawk" held hero status. And I wanted to see the ivy up close and personal. Was it actually the same ivy that was planted in 1937?

After arriving at the White Sox game, my thoughts shifted from the trip we took decades ago to the approaching conclusion to the ballpark tour. I wondered how I would feel walking into the "Friendly Confines," having completed our journey. Would I feel your presence?

Honestly, Mom, it was so hard to keep my attention on the Sox because I knew what was coming up. You'll never believe it. You'd think I made the whole thing up. I wanted to tell you back in my New York letters, when I learned about it for the first time.

Mom, the Chicago Cubs invited me to throw out the first pitch.

Surprise!

Yes, you read that right. I didn't believe it either, the first time I saw the offer appear in my inbox.

I remember being in my New York hotel room when the email arrived from the Cubs. It happened to be the exact same room where you, Rachel, Charlotte, and I stayed when we took a girls' trip to the Big Apple. This time, I sat in the room alone and read: *We would love to host you out here as you visit in September. I'd even like to offer a first pitch to you that day.*

Stunned, I closed my laptop. If I reopened it and the email remained, it must be true. And part of me wanted to experience receiving the email all over again. This time, I viewed the message on my phone. Better to check on different devices, to be certain.

Yep—the Chicago Cubs definitely offered me a first pitch at Wrigley.

What would a normal person do after learning she'd have the opportunity to fulfill a childhood dream? I don't know, but *I* showered. An early morning walk through the city had left me sweaty, and I still wore my workout gear. I thought it would be best to change into more professional attire before I wrote him back. You would have been too busy shrieking and giggling to have thought about bathing!

Within the hour, I made myself look presentable for the sole purpose of sending an email accepting the generous invitation. It felt more official that way. Plus, I do my best thinking in the shower, and perhaps I wanted to savor the news.

I clicked Send, called a few family members and friends to share my excitement, and placed an order for room service. While ordering a glass of wine midday isn't my normal habit, this occasion seemed room-service worthy. Trying to imagine that first pitch, I then did something you would have warned me not to do: I googled it.

Mom! Michael Jordan botched it at Wrigley. The catcher didn't even get a glove on the ball. Nolan Ryan? Not much better. On opening day, one year prior to me leaving for my baseball tour, the Hall-of-Fame pitcher stood on the mound at Minute Maid Park and airmailed it. This left me less than confident and, frankly, terrified. The wine didn't help.

I know what you would have said. "Why did you google it?" Without fail, anytime I told you about a potential love interest, you delivered the same response: "Now don't go searching the internet for everything you can find about him. Leave some mystery in life, Katie. Give a person a chance." In this case, you might have said, "Give yourself a chance."

I've never been a leave-it-up-to-mystery kind of person. The ultimate planner, I preferred to control the outcome. It's one of the many reasons I embarked on this ballpark journey in the first place. I needed to let go. You'd been trying to get me to loosen the reins on control for as long as I can remember.

All the lessons I'd learned about detaching from the outcome and focusing on the present flew out the window of the twenty-first floor of my hotel. *What if I don't even make it to the plate? What if I hit some bystander in the head? What if it goes into the crowd? What if the fans boo me?* And this next thought was the icing on the fear cake I'd baked in my mind: *What if my friends and family spend all that money and time to come see me throw out the first pitch, and I totally screw it up?*

Fear robs us of many things—joy, opportunity, peace of mind, to name a few. In this case, it threatened to rob me of enjoying the White Sox and U.S. Cellular Field. It took the present and practically threw it in the trash. I'm no stranger to missing out on the present because of being so worried about writing the script for the future. I've never been shy about setting excessively high standards for myself. But I knew better now. Or at least I thought I did. Sensing a need to get out of my head, I left my seat at the ballpark and walked around.

That's the beauty of baseball. It quietly lures you back to the present, right when you need it most. I took photographs of the old Comiskey Park shower, relocated from the former home of the White Sox. For decades, it beckoned fans to the outfield concourse on hot summer days. My camera captured a rare slide into first base. I even caught a guy collecting rainwater to refill his bottle. Think of all the things I would have missed if I'd let my old habits consume me.

My favorite photograph of all? A foul ball on the first base line. The fans' and players' reactions seemed to reflect the array of emotions I'd experienced since learning I'd throw out the first pitch.

Some moved toward the foul ball, including the White Sox players who ran into the fence at full steam. At times I, too, ran toward the opportunity I'd been given. "I played softball for fifteen years. I can do this!"

Others ducked. A few weeks after New York, I began practicing. It didn't go well. I hid. "There's no way I can do this."

Many watched with their mouths agape. My same reaction when I queued up YouTube videos of first pitches. "Whoa. *They* couldn't do it?"

All the while, Cleveland's Francisco Lindor, who hit the pop-up, watched the fans and opposing players react. He reminded me of my daily meditations and bearing witness to my anxious and cluttered thoughts.

And a select few kept calm, despite a red-seamed bullet potentially heading straight for their noggins. I especially loved the unflappable grandmother who appeared to trust it would all work out.

I left the ballpark that night knowing exactly which mindset I hoped to embody two weeks later, eight miles north of where I now stood.

XO,
KATIE

BE

DEAR MOM,

I skipped into Wrigley Field, powered by adrenaline, wearing customized Cubs Converse. I swear I could hear Harry Caray's voice echoing between the seats: "*Hello again, everybody. It's a bee-yooo-tiful day for baseball.*" Suddenly, I was back in your room, lying at the end of your bed, my chin perfectly perched on the brass frame. You're sitting in the baby blue recliner, positioned only a couple of feet from the television broadcasting WGN. As usual, you're holding an iced tea with lemon. Harry and his play-by-play announcer, Steve Stone, welcomed us to the telecast and we watch in silence, both hopeful for a Cubbies win.

We always let baseball do the talking, didn't we?

I can't think of a better teacher of how to endure setbacks and loss than the game of baseball. Perhaps no team has suffered more than our lovable losers, the Cubs, who entered the 2015 season on a 108-year World Series win drought. How lucky I am to have completed my journey in Chicago, within the friendly confines and ivy-lined outfield of Wrigley. Many of our friends and family members who supported me through all of life's home runs and strikeouts joined me for this special occasion.

I found a seat behind home plate and watched both teams warm up. While I waited to be called to the field, Phillip Phillips's song "Home" began playing on the ballpark speakers and the hairs on my arms started to dance. Three years earlier, that song was my cancer anthem every time I drove to MD Anderson for radiation. For seventeen days straight, I rolled down Holcomb Avenue in Houston listening to that song and imagining you were with me. It brought me peace when everything in my body was in a state of conflict. That was the sign I needed to realize you had joined me at Wrigley. Thank you for playing it.

From that moment on, you were everywhere. I saw you in the usher's eyes as she told me the story of her sister who died from breast cancer, and then she carefully pinned her sister's cancer ribbon on my jersey. I heard you in the voice of the woman sitting behind us during the game, who said, "Wow, that was a really great throw you made." And I saw you, of course, in all the people who came to support me.

You were there in Melissa's tears as she hugged me,

knowing she witnessed the realization of our long-ago plans. You were there in Michele's loyalty, as she publicized my tour to everyone she met. In Charlotte, I felt your hands, and in Rachel I heard your giggle. In Timmy—your brother and lifetime travel partner—I saw your childlike enthusiasm. While Dad couldn't join us (you knew better than anyone he didn't like baseball or flying much), he was definitely rooting me on from New Orleans. And don't worry, I made sure Andre Dawson was there too. I proudly wore number 8. I had a feeling I would need some of the Hawk's quiet resolve when I took the mound.

I remember wishing Ella was with us. You won't believe it, but a call with her later in the week revealed she also was in Chicago that night! Traveling by train from Mississippi to Milwaukee to visit her sister, Ella's train stopped in Chicago around the same time I threw out the first pitch. Wishes do come true, don't they?

I couldn't have completed the journey without a long cast of characters, including Peyton. Remember our neighbors from across the street? He and I had big dreams in our Seventh Street yard. He would throw the football with his brothers and dream of being an NFL quarterback like his dad. And in that same yard, when no one was watching, I would act out critical game-winning pitches, dreaming of being on the mound at Wrigley. Fast-forward thirty years, Peyton's dream had long since come true, and he read about my baseball odyssey. As he has done for countless others, he made my childhood dream come true.

Thanks to my childhood friend, that night I walked to the mound and took it all in—the smell of the grass, the crisp fall Chicago air, the buzz of the fans eagerly taking their seats. The grounds crew hydrated the field one last time underneath the scoreboard where "Katie Russell, Guest of the Cubs" appeared in bright lights. You would have been so proud.

I finally understood what you meant when you would tell me, "Let go, Katie—just be." For the previous twenty-nine ballparks, that's what I did. I tried to be with the fans and listen to the stories of all the people whose paths I crossed. I tried to be present and immerse myself in each new community. I tried to be with my child self, my adult self, and the self I longed to be.

I stepped onto the mound that night with all of this in mind. When the crowd grew silent and the breeze ceased, all I could see was the catcher. It was me and Dad playing catch on the front porch of Seventh Street. It was me and the white brick wall in the backyard. I stared down the sixty feet six inches and raised my glove in front of my face so I could take one last deep breath in private. As I lowered it, I cocked my right arm back and launched the ball in the air, making sure to follow through. "The follow-through is the most important part," you once told me.

In the end, I knew it didn't matter where the ball landed. I had learned to detach from outcomes—cancer has a way of coaching you to do that. Mainly, though, I didn't want to write my own ending. Often our stories have a better ending than we could ever dream up for ourselves. Six months prior, I couldn't have imagined that my journey would end with me standing on the mound at Wrigley.

Mom, I know how competitive you were. Wherever you're reading this, you're probably wondering what happened after the ball left my hand. Your eyes were no doubt closed up there in heaven when I began my pitching motion. But I didn't practice all those years in the backyard for nothing. The ball landed right in the catcher's mitt. As he and I jogged toward each other, he handed me the ball, looked right into my eyes, and said, "You nailed it." I didn't have the heart to tell him he was wrong.

We nailed it, Mom.

XO,
KATIE

EPILOGUE: EXTRA INNINGS

OCTOBER 2016

BE Patient

MOM!

I know you were there. The Cubs made it to the World Series for the first time in seventy-one years and you wouldn't miss it. Were you hiding in the outfield ivy? Floating in right field near Jason Heyward and our old bleacher seats? Or were you in the press box, drinking a cold one with Harry?

Did you see me?

On Melissa's fortieth birthday and one week before I, too, turned forty, we were given tickets for seats on the lower level, third base side. Before the game started, I tracked down the usher from last year's visit to Wrigley. I wanted to show her I still wore her sister's breast cancer baseball pin on my jacket. We hugged and chatted briefly so she could return to her post. She felt like family.

Melissa and I found our seats early, ensuring we didn't miss any of the pregame action, especially the national anthem. Game Four of the World Series was a special night at the ballpark, dedicated to honoring those impacted by cancer. A Stand Up to Cancer sign rested atop our seats, awaiting our arrival. The placards read, "I Stand Up For," with either a blank space for people to write in a name of their choice or a space already filled in with a group impacted by cancer. Those groups included loved ones, those we've lost, those in the fight, and caregivers. The one placed on my seat read "survivors."

At the end of the fifth inning, Joe Buck, the Fox Sports announcer for the game, asked everyone in the ballpark to stand and hold up their signs. It appeared as if everyone had

forgone their between-inning hot dogs and bathroom runs to partake—fans, umpires, players, coaches, concession vendors, camera crews, and television announcers all raised signs.

Behind each sign stood a person with a story. Thinking about the forty-one-thousand–plus stories of love and loss contained in the historic ballpark brought me to tears. And I thought about my cancer journey and what it took for me to be standing in Wrigley Field, holding up a cancer survivor sign. I thought about Melissa and how she lost her boyfriend to leukemia on her twenty-third birthday—this exact night seventeen years ago. And we both probably thought about you, Mom. Without you, this lifelong love affair with the Cubs never would have begun. I realized in that fifteen seconds of stillness that we're all connected by this awful disease and no one is immune from its impact.

Four innings later, Cleveland closed out Game Four with the win. Doubt filled the ballpark, and the Cubs fans exited in a decidedly less-spirited fashion than when they'd entered. A World Series win seemed improbable. I buttoned up my jacket to ward off what felt like a sudden drop in temperature, as a gust of wind whipped through the stands. I believed it was you whispering, *"Be patient, Katie. This is not over."* I left the ballpark disappointed—Cubs down 3–1 and Cleveland one game away from clinching—but with a twinge of hope that seemed to be percolating deep inside, underneath my Cubs vintage Starter jacket.

How could I not have hope? It had been 108 years since the Cubs won a World Series—the longest championship drought in American sports. The digits 1, 0, and 8 appeared everywhere, offering signs *this* would be the year. The distance from both the left field and right field foul poles to home plate at Wrigley Field—108 meters. The number of stitches on a baseball—108. The last two Cubs players to be inducted into the Hall of Fame? Ron Santo (#10) and my favorite player of all time, Andre Dawson (#8). The very first Cubs World Series game held at Wrigley? October 8, 1929 (10/8).

Everyone seemed to have some tie to the number 108. Mine? I'd spent the past four years cultivating a meditation and yoga practice. Around my neck I'd worn a mala necklace strung with prayer beads, precisely 108 of them.

Cleveland didn't clinch the series in Chicago the next night. Game Five ended with a Cubs victory, and this time fans stayed in the ballpark long after the game concluded. We sang and danced. "Go Cubs Go! Go Cubs Go! Hey, Chicago, what do you say? The Cubs are gonna win today!" We flew our white flags adorned with blue Ws. Hoisting the Commissioner's Trophy would require two road wins. The odds remained low but, on that night, hope ran high.

I thought back to when I took the mound at the end of the 2015 season. Thirteen months earlier, I never would have imagined watching Aroldis Chapman toe that same rubber to close out a Game Five win—the first World

Series win at Wrigley since 1945. Something else I never imagined? Fist-bumping with actor Bill Murray before taking a photo of our matching custom Cubs Converse.

The Cubs found a way to force a Game Seven. Friends offered various opportunities to watch the deciding game, including a trip to Progressive Field in Cleveland. Some hosted parties at their homes, Super Bowl style. Others invited me to watch at a bar sure to be filled with Austinites dressed in the preferred C logo and my favored hues of blue and red.

I declined all invitations, stayed at home, and watched on the couch by myself.

Honestly, I wanted to be that little girl in your bedroom— just you and me, Mom. I made iced tea, with lemon of course, like you always did. I imagined you giddy one moment then serious the next, sitting on the edge of the La-Z-Boy recliner with your elbows on your knees, leaning into the broadcast. Nervous, you would have turned your head away from the television often, saying, "I can't look." The game evoked every emotion in me. I cheered. I panicked. I laughed. I yelled. I prayed. I snacked. Mainly, I cried. A lot.

I think many of the fans in heaven joined me in crying too. For seventeen minutes, in between the ninth and tenth innings, their collective tears caused the first-ever rain delay in a Game Seven of a World Series.

Divine intervention? You wouldn't know anything about that, would you?

The players stayed patient in the locker room, led by their manager, Joe Maddon, who'd responded to pressure all year with fun. When the tenth inning began, the Cubs' designated hitter, Kyle Schwarber, stood at the plate with the score tied 6–6. He'd torn his ACL and LCL in the third game of the season and waited patiently all year to return to the lineup. Rumor had it, he spent much of his rehab standing in the batter's box, watching an arsenal of pitches whiz by for hours. Never swinging a bat, training his eye so that when the time came, he'd be ready. His lead-off single started a two-run tenth inning for the Cubs.

Chicago would win 8–7, to become the World Series champions for the first time in 108 years! In 10 innings, 8 runs. Coincidence?

I sprung off the couch, threw my arms in the air, and began the loudest foot-stomping, hand-clapping celebration a one-woman band could muster. My phone lit up with text messages from fellow fans and banner alerts from every sporting news outlet in the world. And then came another round of tears.

I cried out of joy for all the current and former players and coaches who'd waited for this improbable day to arrive.

I cried for the die-hard fans (like you and me) who never gave up on the lovable losers.

I cried because I wished you were with me to celebrate, because cancer took you from me too soon, because I had to imagine your reaction instead of hearing it.

I cried for the little girl in the backyard on Seventh Street, who spent much of her life scared and anxious but found a way to live out her dream despite the many obstacles along the way.

I cried for the pain of cancer, the fear, the falling down, the time I cried out for God on the bathroom floor, not knowing if I'd live.

I cried because in three days, I'd say goodbye to my thirties—a decade that brought me heartache and pain but also a lot of joy and wisdom.

Everything changed that day. Everyone knew that. No matter where you watched or how long you'd been a Cubs or baseball fan, this was a defining moment in sports history and a defining moment for a franchise that had long been loved, not in spite of, but because of, its losing identity. Who would they become now that they were winners? What kind of fans would you and I be, Mom, now that our perpetual underdogs were no more? Where do I go from here, now that my baseball journey had its perfect ending?

I'm not entirely sure. And I'm okay with that.

So let it be.

XO,

KATIE

NOVEMBER 2018

BE Love

OKAY, OKAY—YOU WERE RIGHT, MOM!

I fell in love.

It may have taken me 6 months, more than 270 innings, and over 30,000 miles, but I got the message you were trying to tell me all those years ago.

I said yes to baseball, and I fell in love with the game all over again.

I fell for all the little things in baseball that set it apart from other sports. There's no clock. Some argue it's too slow, that it doesn't hold people's interest in today's world of instant gratification. I disagree. I fell in love with the pace of baseball because it forced me to be still. In moments, it can be so quiet you can hear the universe whispering. The lessons, however, speak loudly—both those from the game and from its fans. Baseball taught me how to really listen to those around me and, most importantly, to my own voice.

I said yes to your dream of seeing all thirty MLB ballparks, and I fell in love with you.

Isn't it strange that the loss of someone heightens her presence? It took your absence to understand you and your gifts. I spent so much of my life trying to be nothing like you. Now, I appreciate the unwavering love of life you demonstrated daily with your spontaneous, carefree, jump-at-every-adventure attitude. I hope to emulate it as I navigate this unpredictable world without you. Your parenting was not stereotypical or ordinary, but it was pure and unconditional. Thank you for choosing to be my mom.

I said yes to me, and I learned how to love the person staring back from the mirror.

I went in search of you, Mom, and I found myself. It is because of you and baseball (and truckloads of therapy) that this anxiety-ridden, fearful kid I have known for most of my life finally feels worthy of love. I've begun to understand the complex formula for loving all of me, even with the many scars and the mistakes I've made. The wounds weren't completely my fault, but the healing from them was, and always will be, my responsibility. There is still work to be done, and my fears still exist, especially when a pain arises and I wonder if it's a sign that I'm sick again. But I don't run from fear anymore. I sit with it. I learn from it. And I use its message to guide my choices and life decisions.

As soon as I became comfortable with who I am and what I wanted, wouldn't you know it—I began to attract the exact right things in my life. Because I said yes to baseball, to you, and to myself, I will say yes to an amazing man. You have never met him, but I am certain you have known about him all along.

In late February 2018, a phone call to Rachel and an admission that I was ready to find my person led me to do something I never thought I would: I joined a dating app called Bumble. I spent that entire day, sunup to sundown, texting Rachel back and forth, trying to capture the right words and photographs to describe Katie Russell. Not the person you knew when you were alive but rather the Katie Russell you knew I was capable of becoming.

I published my profile, including the picture of me at Wrigley, and began swiping—right if I was interested, left if I wasn't. "Oohs" and "ahhs" accompanied some swipes, screenshots others. Before I knew it, a whole slew of matches appeared. Overwhelmed, I decided to write to only three people. I kept coming back to a man named Brand. I said to Rachel, "He looks kind. Oh, and by the way, he's wearing a Cubs hat. That one. That's the one I want to talk to first."

Unbeknownst to Brand and me, fate was already working its magic.

In 2016, before Game Four of the World Series, Brand joined hundreds of fans in front of the Wrigley Field marquee to take a photograph. Hours later, Melissa snapped a photo of me in front of the same iconic front door to the Friendly Confines. Brand and I had traveled to Chicago to be part of the historic World Series; I flew from Austin and he drove from Iowa. We had (unknowingly) crossed paths.

Our paths inched closer thirteen months later when we flew separately to Cabo San Lucas to celebrate our birthdays at the exact same time in November. Much of the conversation between Brand and his friend that weekend centered on one topic. (Was Brand going to move to Austin?)

Meanwhile, Annie (my travel wife) and I sat poolside drinking margaritas. With conviction and a mouthful of ceviche, I turned to her and said, "Mark my words. I am going to get married here." No man in sight, but whoever he was, I knew I would return with him one day.

Monday morning after entering the Bumble world, I decided to write Brand. Naturally, I ran my potential text by Rachel; her husband; two friends; a coworker; my neighbor's dog, Waylon; and the red bird that perched on my balcony. *Hi Brand! Where did you move from?* Looking back, I'm disappointed in my lack of creativity. And what was my posse thinking when they told me that was a good idea? His response included where he'd lived previously and ended with, *More importantly, tell me about that Cubs picture!* And the love story began. Four days later we met up for happy hour, and I was smitten. One week later, I deleted the app. I had found my person.

Mom, you tried Chicago and Cabo and who knows how many other ways to bring us together. In the end, life's twists and turns led me right into Brand Alexander Newland's loving arms.

Your cancer.
My cancer.
The loss of our home.

The baseball journey.
You.
All of it.

Through everything, I've learned that an imperfect life can be beautiful, just like the imperfect game of baseball. There will always be strikeouts and slumps, but if you keep showing up in the batter's box and swinging away, the home runs will eventually come. It took forty-one years, but I finally hit a grand slam when I met Brand.

The Cubs won the World Series, there's been a report of pigs flying in the area, and yes, Mom, I'm getting married. Whether you float by butterfly or atop the waves flowing from the gulf to the Pacific, I'll be waiting for you in Baja, Mexico—the place where we took our last trip together before your cancer diagnosis.

You don't have to be a ballplayer to experience the magic of baseball. I am proof that if you love the game, the game will love you back.

Just like life.

XO,
KATIE

BE Flexible

Dear Mom,

We canceled our dream wedding in Mexico.

Instead of friends and family joining us in Baja, where the mountains meet the sea, instead of poolside chats and chips, instead of wedding-night toasts with tequila, everyone stayed at home and self-quarantined. Coronavirus arrived in the United States and, with it, the declaration of a global pandemic.

The Mexico and United States border closed the day we had planned to fly to our destination wedding. By that time, the wedding had long been called off. We worried about our at-risk guests, including your brother and sister-in-law and several others with autoimmune diseases. We worried that we could potentially bring the virus to the beautiful people of Todos Santos. While government officials reported no cases of COVID-19 in Baja at the time, our intuition and conscience spoke loudly: *It's the socially responsible thing to do.*

NBA players left the courts, PGA golfers deserted the greens, NHL skaters stored their sticks, and MLB's commissioner shut down spring training. No tennis shoe squeaks, no driver *thwacks*, and no more cracks of the bats meant no major-league sports appeared on our screens. Perhaps even sadder, the NCAA canceled its March Madness tournament, meaning most seniors unknowingly had played the last games of their careers. You and I loved watching a bracket bust and a buzzer-beating shot lift an underdog to the top.

I especially missed baseball.

Historically, baseball had been a source of comfort for society during tough times. Baseball boosted morale during wars as families suffered emotionally, physically, and financially. After 9/11, fans turned to postseason baseball to distract them from their anxiety and fear. Play even continued during part of the 1918 Spanish flu, offering hope to those with family members afflicted.

And baseball saved me countless times.

It saved me from boredom during hot and sticky New Orleans summers, and it rescued me from boyfriend break-ups. It provided an escape in 2012, when I sheltered in place with cancer. It saved us during hurricanes, especially the time you came to visit me because the storm washed away your home.

Baseball, my source of healing during times of struggle, couldn't save me from my canceled wedding or COVID-19. Not this time.

But here's what did: all of the lessons I've learned over the last forty-three years from life and from you.

When our childhood home vanished into the gulf, I learned how to let go of material things. When I vomited for hours because my body rejected the cancer drugs, I learned that my faith remained strong. When you died, I learned that life is fragile and never guaranteed.

Without you and baseball, I wondered who or what would give me hope.

Turns out, Brand and I created our own. I no longer needed hindsight to see that even in the disappointment of our cancelled wedding, an opportunity existed.

On a gray and drizzly morning in Austin, Texas, we walked hand in hand to the home of a retired judge. Brand sported a navy-blue suit, and I wore an ivory Mexican-themed maxi dress. The judge opened the door to his home and then his folio.

"Being a judge means doing unpleasant things, but adoptions and weddings have brought me great joy over the years."

We took our places in front of his oversize, cobble-stone fireplace—the type you find in a cabin buried deep in the woods. A Christmas wreath and antlers hung above, and his family members watched from the picture frames perched on the wooden mantle. If they looked closely, they would've seen beads of sweat percolating through Brand's skin. Perhaps an indication of the magnitude of the moment or, more likely, because of his formal attire on a hot, humid spring day. I wondered if you might be there, adding to our guest list of one. An unseasonal scarecrow resting against the corner wall of the living room did catch my eye, but I decided you'd have dressed more appropriately for the occasion.

A declaration. Rings slid on sweaty fingers. A kiss. Some judge-requested selfies. And five minutes later, Brand and Katie Newland were official.

We strolled to the park next door, and on the luckiest day of the year (according to the Irish), Brand and I stood in the overgrown grass, shared our vows, and danced our first dance to "Bless the Broken Road" by Rascal Flatts.

I'd written my vows months earlier, but the ending seemed particularly fitting given the circumstances:

"Being grateful for where I am in this very moment inherently means that I am thankful for the long and winding road that got me here. For all the roads we have walked to get here and for all the roads to come, may we walk together, hand in hand, guided by love and light."

The sun peeked through the clouds. We hand sanitized. And our phones buzzed from an incoming tweet. *Effective immediately, all bars and restaurants in Austin will be closed to the public except for to-go or curbside orders.* We pivoted, as we had done so many times already that week. We scrapped our celebratory lunch and opted for a takeout pizza.

Over wine and slices, we played a baseball board game and reflected on our park wedding. We recalled the trees that stood in as our guests, witnessing our promise to love each other forever.

Like the trunk rings scientists use to learn more about the conditions a tree experienced during its lifetime (narrow rings representing disease or drought), all of us will carry the ring of 2020. The year of the virus. The year of canceling weddings and baseball. The year of canceling everything.

And if scientists ever decide to examine our rings, they'll find our wedding bands secured to our fingers—an enduring sign of patience, hope, and, most importantly, love.

While this wasn't the ending to my letters for you that I'd imagined, or the beginning of married life I'd envisioned, the lesson learned was clear.

No matter how hard we try to write our story, the story ends up writing itself.

XO,

KATIE

———————————————

Acknowledgments

N o one lives out their dreams alone. *A Season with Mom* exists because of my amazing teammates who have supported me throughout my life. This book reflects the voices and perspectives of the many teachers, family members, and friends who have graciously shared their time and wisdom with me.

To the Harper Horizon team who welcomed me with open arms and gave my story a home . . .

Andrea Fleck-Nisbet, for investing in a first-time author. Amanda Bauch, for championing me and my writing. Your encouragement and editing expertise are unmatched. John Andrade, Kayleigh Hines, Belinda Bass, and Denise Froehlich, for all of your behind-the-scenes work that brought this book to life in the most magical way. I am grateful to all of you for nurturing this book into the world.

To my agent, Kristin van Ogtrop, who had me at hello. Thank you for believing in me. Your quick wit, honest feedback, and genuine love of books and life made the publishing process a joy. I am lucky to have you in my dugout and to call you a friend.

⚾ ⚾ ⚾

To my family, who didn't have a choice in picking me but continue to choose me every day . . .

Dad, for giving selflessly and modeling compassion daily. Hugh, for being an empathetic listener. Molly, for reminding me that with determination I can accomplish anything. Charlotte, for always showing up for me. Benjie, for making me laugh even when I didn't feel like it. Rachel, for being the little sister I have always looked up to.

Alec, Matt, Gabi, James, Bryce, Alexis, Taylor, Hunter, Hagan, Grace, and Annie, for being the bright future of our family. May this book bring you closer to your grandmother and to a part of you.

And, Mom, for your strength, for your wisdom, and for instilling in me a love of baseball and life. Your fingerprints are all over these pages. Because of you, I will forever root for the underdog.

⚾ ⚾ ⚾

To those I consider family and who have welcomed me into theirs . . .

Ella, for loving me as if I were her own. It is your kind soul that I try to emulate every day.

Melissa, otherwise known as the seventh Russell child, for being a part of every big and small moment in my life. You have always been and will always be family.

Charles, for your unwavering love and support. There are no words to describe the indelible impact you have had on me. Your generosity of spirit and assiduous efforts to help others will forever guide my life's work.

⚾ ⚾ ⚾

To all my friends, who continuously cheer me on, even when I strike out . . .

Michele, for always championing me without hesitation. Your loyalty and steadfast commitment to your friends is a gift to all who know you. I am grateful we are on the same team.

Audra, for all of your literary and life wisdom that informed this book. My writing became stronger because of you. Thank you for being my weekly writing buddy and teaching partner for all these years.

Carl, for all of your sports analogies that helped me process every valley and peak in my life. Without your confidence in me, I might never have found my own.

⚾ ⚾ ⚾

To those who supported me in my quest to see all thirty MLB ballparks . . .

Peyton, for giving this baseball-loving kid a chance to fulfill a dream. While your name will forever be remembered in the football record books, perhaps your greatest accomplishment is what you've done for others off the field.

Kate Norton, Angie Zapata, Bridget and John Bentley, Steph Giroux, Melissa Olson, Christina Russell, Diane Bauhof, and Jennifer Broom, for taking time out of your busy schedules to join me for a game.

Bridget Bentley, Sarah Weisman, Beth and Mustaque Ali, Melissa Ehlinger, Michele Bell, Tim and Claire Avegno, Liz Kirk, Demi Brand, Robert and Olga Castañeda, Georgina Podjenski, Charles Butt, Charlotte Bradford, Hugh Russell, Rachel Krenz, Benjie Russell, Thomas Keaty, Rob Waechter, Dan and Trish Schumacher, Mandy and Aman Johnson, and Bill and Kate Norton, for making the trek to Chicago to witness my childhood dream come true.

Steve Cohen, Sarah Scott, UT Baseball, Jason Kershner, and Matthew Odam, for cheering me on from afar and who played an important role in my journey.

Cassy Weyandt, for sharing your photographic expertise and your enthusiasm for my story.

Sage Billick, for inviting me into your home and into your community.

Aman Johnson, for capturing the essence of my story through your lens.

⊘ ⊘ ⊘

To the faculty and students in the College of Education at the University of Texas at Austin, in the Department of Education at Trinity University, and at Isidore Newman School, for teaching me what it means to be a lifelong learner.

To my cancer team at MD Anderson—Lizabeth McCall, Loven Paynes, Dr. Nathan Fowler, Elizabeth Sorensen, Dr. Bouthaina Dabaja, Dr. Randal Weber, Dr. Gottumukkala Raju, and Dr. John Stroehlein—for taking such good care of me so I could live long enough to make this book a reality. I am indebted to you and all of the nurses, technicians, and staff at MD Anderson who impacted my healing. My cancer never stood a chance with you all as my teammates.

⊘ ⊘ ⊘

To Brand Alexander Newland, for choosing me. This book would never have been written if it weren't for your steady way of being and the unconditional love you surround me with every day. In you, I found my lifetime baseball-watching partner. Thank you for giving me my happy ending and the beginning of a whole new chapter.

About the Author

K atie Russell Newland is a writer and sports enthusiast with a PhD in language and literacy from the University of Texas at Austin. A survivor of both Hodgkin's lymphoma and melanoma, she is now in remission and lives with her family in Austin, Texas. When she's not watching sports or her favorite teams play (Chicago Cubs, New Orleans Saints, and Texas Longhorns), she can be found attending a music festival, hosting a board game night, or playing pickleball. Katie's story has been featured by ESPN, *People*, *Good Morning America*, *Today*, *Condé Nast Traveler*, and the *Huffington Post*.